LEADERSHIP
STARTS
HERE

STEVE LISHANSKY

Published by Optimize Leadership Publishing.
Printed in the United States of America

ISBN: 978-1-7367043-2-5 Paperback

Book cover design by Rose Davies
Book design by Dave Vasudevan

This publication is designed to provide accurate and authoritative information in regard to the subject matter covered. It is sold with the understanding that the publisher is not engaged in rendering legal, accounting, or other professional services. If legal advice or other expert assistance is required, the services of a competent professional person should be sought.

LEADERSHIP STARTS HERE

"When you change the way you look at things,
The things you look at change."
Max Planck (Nobel Prize Physicist)

INTRODUCTION

Have you ever really considered the question: Where does leadership start?

The importance, influence, and impact of leadership means this is a significant question.

This book is dedicated to answering that question – and providing you with what it takes to enhance your leadership impact and results.

I say that leadership start with your decisions. Everything starts with your decisions.

Just as important – your decisions start with your decision-making process. The quality of your leadership decision-making process is the most fundamental starting point for massively impacting, accelerating, and elevating your team, business, and organization – and your life.

This book is about the decision-making process that transforms how leaders generate clarity, focus, and impact on what is most important and valuable. This process – conducted well – ensures that everything that flows from these decisions provides the most effective foundation for sustainable growth, culture development, execution, and success.

You are cordially invited on this journey to greater clarity, better focus, increased impact, and ultimately the maximum leverage for getting your organization to be the best it can be.

(Note: everything here works for your life, family, community – every dimension of life – as well…)

I wish you great growth, success, and fulfillment!
Steve Lishansky
Boston, MA
May 2021

TABLE OF CONTENTS

SECTION 1

LEADERSHIP STARTS HERE

*"The distance between the leader and the average is a constant.
If leadership performance is high, the average will go up.
It is easier to raise the performance of one leader than it is
to raise the performance of a whole mass."*
Peter Drucker

"Imagine if you could raise the performance of a team of leaders..."
Steve Lishansky

CHAPTER 1

LEADERSHIP AND DECISION-MAKING

*"Simple, clear purpose and principles give rise to
complex and intelligent behavior.
Complex rules and regulations give rise
to simple and stupid behaviors."*
Dee Hoch (Founder of VISA)

At the most fundamental level, leadership requires clear and effective decisions – **especially about what is most important and valuable to focus on and act on.** It also requires the collective ownership of, commitment to, and alignment of your team and organization with these most critically important decisions.

When we are looking at improving an organization's performance and results, the first and fastest question to gauge how well its leadership decision-making process is working is: "How strategically aligned is your leadership team?"

This is really asking whether what is most important and valuable is clear, agreed upon, collectively owned, fully pursued, and implemented.

For a high functioning leader and organization, dealing with today's continuously changing and challenging internal and external environments, is there a single question more important to answer – especially for knowing how your leadership team is working?

Smart leaders know that the quality of your leadership team's decision-making process, decisions, and the alignment around those decisions has everything to do with the quality of your organization's performance and results.

Learning how well aligned your leadership team's decision-making process and decisions are can be uncovered in *less than 30 minutes*. A set of 3 simple questions, asked one-on-one of each of the organization's senior leaders, reveals what needs to be known.

How consistent and well aligned their answers are will immediately tell you the following critically important information:

- What they really think is most important and valuable to focus on
- What the focus of their attention, time, and resources really is
- Where the divergences among your leaders are
- How effective your leadership decision-making process is
- How much agreement and alignment your top people have around the key drivers of results and success
- How much collaboration and commitment to mutual success really exists
- Ultimately, what decisions are driving the organization

This simple yet highly effective 3-question process that any organization can use typically produces results that are anywhere from sobering to scary. Try it yourself with your top people and see if your results are consistent with what has been found with organizations around the world.

Here are the questions to be asked of each person, individually, one-on-one:

- What is our organization's 3-year Vision?
- What is our organization's Mission?
- What are our organization's top 3 strategic Objectives this year?

THE STARTING POINT

These are such simple questions – yet the quality and alignment of the answers that your people provide are critical to the success of your organization. One big challenge leaders face is that these specific questions and their answers are often missed, ignored, or not even considered as you attempt to move forward with your current strategies. However, missing strong, high quality answers means you miss the starting point for creating the best and most successful outcomes – and achieving them in the most effective and efficient way.

Missing agreement and alignment on the answers to these questions indicates that your underlying decision-making process is weak or flawed. It also means you have found a key culprit for many of the problems and under-achievement of your organization.

Your decision-making process – and the effectiveness of the decisions that flow from it – are the starting points and foundation for the clarity and focus that produces the greatest impact and results. The best and most effective decisions create extreme clarity about what really matters – and why they matter as critical priorities. That in turn enables a quality of focus by your people that produces better choices and results, and does it faster.

That is the structure and process of decision-making that I call the Strategic Alignment Process™. **It produces clarity about what is most important, why those choices are the best ones, and how to produce results that really matter.**

Yet, amazingly enough and sorry to say, a high-quality decision-making process is usually missing – especially on teams, in groups, and in organizations. **The ultimate power of a team or organization should be to multiply the impact and results possible** by bringing talented people together.

However, the impact of a group can be detrimental to success, because a weak or inadequate decision-making process inevitably results in poor quality choices. The resulting lack of clarity about agreed upon priorities – and lack of a compelling rationale for why the decisions made are the best possible decisions – reduces performance and results way below what you would hope for and should expect.

It does not have to be this way!

Consider that the answers to these 3 simple questions must be addressed as the foundations of a high-quality decision-making process. They are the drivers of all your other critical decisions, actions, and measurements of success.

Among many other nasty symptoms, missing a high-quality decision-making process is the leading cause of:

⟡ Time-consuming meetings that go too long, do too little, never address what really matters, and produce little to no progress

⟡ Massive action and activities that at the end of the day (week, month, quarter, year) produce highly insufficient results for all the talent, effort, and resources employed

⟡ Fractured communication that confuses more than clarifies what really matters

⟡ Misalignment of priorities due to lack of agreement around the most important organizational priorities

⟡ Silo mentalities driven by continuously poor decision-making and misalignment

⟡ A "strategy du jour" effect, where priorities seem to change every day

⟡ Blame and finger-pointing for the mistakes and misses that keep happening

⟡ Conflict and recrimination as people justify their lack of success with excuses and rationalizations – because they don't even know what started the train of events going downhill

Every one of us who have ever spent time inside organizations has seen these issues.

Transforming these poisons that threaten outstanding organizational progress, productivity, and performance is achievable – and why this book exists!

Leadership starts by focusing your people on what really matters, inspiring them with why that matters, and developing the best strategies for moving your organization forward. Your decision-making process and the decisions that flow from it are where this all starts.

As Archimedes said: "Give me a lever long enough and a place to stand, and I can move the world."

In your hands are the keys to the Strategic Alignment Process™. This is the simplest, fastest, most efficient, and effective process for defining and building agreement and alignment around the most critical decision-making factors. These principles, practices, and skills are your lever – when you use them well. The Strategic Alignment Process™ spells out how to recognize and position yourself and your people to stand in the best place to move your world.

Use these Strategic Alignment Process™ principles and practices well and you have your launching pad for:

✧ Effective decision-making
✧ Higher quality leadership effectiveness
✧ Abundant organizational results
✧ Accomplishments at a speed and quality that will dazzle you

CHAPTER 2

WHY DECISION-MAKING IS SO CHALLENGING

"Inability to make decisions is one of the principle reasons executives fail. Deficiency in decision-making ranks much higher than lack of specific knowledge or technical know-how as an indicator of leadership failure."

John C. Maxwell

Everyone complains about the poor processes, inefficiencies, challenges, and lack of speed in decision-making so often found in organizations. Yet so few leaders make a concerted and effective effort to address the underlying dynamics that cause these issues.

Quality decisions are what your people want to support their efficiency in action and overall effectiveness, as well as their ultimate success and results. **When were you taught about the dynamics of decision-making?**

When did you learn, develop, or employ a highly reliable decision-making process you, your team, and your organization can consistently turn to, rely on, and utilize for superior focus, choices, and results?

Almost everyone who answers this question says they were never educated about decision-making dynamics and principles. It is no wonder that the foundation of everything that we value is lacking clarity, focus, and success.

Some of the insidious, nasty, negative results of a poor decision-making process and the resulting lack of Strategic Alignment include:

- ✧ Lack of quality results
- ✧ Lack of engagement by your people
- ✧ Lack of teamwork – along with blame or avoidance
- ✧ Lack of communication
- ✧ Lack of leadership
- ✧ Lack of trust in leadership, colleagues, teamwork
- ✧ Lack of well-integrated cooperation and collaboration
- ✧ Lack of focus on the most important and valuable issues and opportunities
- ✧ Lack of quality client relationships and responsiveness to your initiatives
- ✧ Lack of consistent organizational growth and improvement

Too often decision-making takes place in a vacuum. That means that a process for the best and most effective decisions is often weak or missing completely. This occurs for a number of very significant, dangerous, and disruptive reasons – and these often combine to cause even greater havoc, disarray, and diversion of attention, focus, resources, and results.

WARNING SIGNS OF A POOR DECISION-MAKING PROCESS

Below is a list of more than 30 of the most common causes of poor decision-making. However, we know that **the premier cause of poor decision-making is a poor decision-making process.**

Go through this list and see how many are common to your teams. Remember that awareness is the first step to positive change. Poor process leads to these causes of poor decision-making – and the source of most of the failures in your organization. Among the most important warning signs of a poor process leading to problems include:

1. Lack of focus and poor decision-making due to an inadequate, missing, poorly defined, or questionable Vision or Mission
2. Lack of defining what the most important and valuable priorities are to achieve ultimate success
3. Lack of clarity about why what are claimed to be most important are actually the best possible choices
4. Lack of alignment between the stated Goals and how they are connecting to fulfilling a meaningful Mission and Vision
5. Lack of accountability for delivering on the most important priorities
6. Lack of perspective on how to validate that the most appropriate and important choices are being made and revised as required
7. Demand for speed and activity without clarity about why it would be valuable for achieving the most meaningful results
8. Hierarchical acquiescence – do what the boss says, even when it makes no sense
9. Focus on activity rather than results – where being busy and in action obscures the importance of producing meaningful and valuable results
10. Lack of focus on what is most important for progress and success
11. Lack of prioritizing – including the ability to re-prioritize as required
12. Everything is a top priority – so in effect nothing is really THE priority
13. Poor metrics and benchmarks to identify progress
14. Lack of thinking
15. Lack of responsibility for decisions
16. Thinking you are meant to be problem solving instead of achieving key results
17. Following every issue "down the rabbit hole" instead of deciding which ones are priorities that deserve attention and action

18. Gossiping instead of speaking to the person or people involved
19. Lack of input from key people who could be valuable in the decision-making process
20. Lack of training on how to make better decisions – individually and in teams
21. Poor communication – which is often one of the key reasons for not being clear about what decisions are important
22. Cheap answers to insignificant questions
23. Fear of rejection or reaction
24. Poorly planned meetings that lack clarity and focus
25. Poor communication of important decisions people need to be aware of
26. Substantive conversations going on outside the decision-making process that add nothing to the quality of the decision
27. Missing critical information necessary to make a quality decision
28. Making decisions without utilizing available, important, meaningful, and relevant information
29. Waiting too long for information to the point the decisions won't have timeliness, relevance, impact, or value
30. Failing to understand why prior decisions did or did not work out well
31. Blaming people to the point they fear making decisions or taking responsibility
32. Pushing decisions "up the chain of command" to the point where decision-makers are too far removed from critical information to make good decisions
33. Lack of Strategic Alignment – meaning that members of your leadership team are pulling in different directions, focusing on different priorities and results

These are all obvious symptoms of a poor, incoherent, messy, unclear, or just incompetent decision-making process. Of course, you can easily see what happens when the foundations of decision-making are weak and Strategic Alignment is missing. Everything accelerates its inevitable slide downhill, causing slow-downs and havoc in pursuit of your results and making life among your people a painful and difficult experience.

Are you ready to transform these scenarios? Are you ready to inspire and ignite the engagement, passion, and capabilities of your people with a great decision-making process?

A high-quality decision-making process elevates every part of your organization, providing a foundation you can launch great and worthy results from.

Let's build that now!

CHAPTER 3

WHAT THE BEST LEADERS HAVE AND DO

"Management is doing things right;
Leadership is doing the right things."
Peter Drucker

How well have you considered these important questions about leadership performance?

◇ What has to happen to build the critical foundations for planning, action, execution, client relationships, talent development, building culture, and delivering results?

◇ What does it take to build these foundations effectively?

◇ What differentiates the best and most successful leaders from average and under-performing leaders?

◇ Where do I start to accelerate and elevate our leadership performance and results?

Too many leaders express satisfaction with their organizational performance – until they see what others are achieving in the same marketplace. Too many executives are satisfied when they can hit their numbers – regardless of whether or not doing that:

◇ Reflects the best short- and long-term choices to grow the organization

◇ Defines sustainable and sound results that make sense

✧ Offers clarity of objectives that people can focus on and deliver successfully

✧ Moves their organization, colleagues, and clients forward in meaningful ways

✧ Frees the leadership team members and their people with minimal oversight and direction

A top-performing leader is always asking these 9 critical leadership questions:

1. How do we get better every year?
2. How do we continue to grow our people, productivity, performance, and profitability?
3. What would make the biggest difference in producing our most important improvements and advances?
4. What is working best?
5. Are we fully leveraging these success factors and strengths that are working best?
6. What is most challenging?
7. Are we effectively mitigating these challenging issues and obstacles?
8. Does everyone clearly understand what is most important – for them, their teams, and our organization?
9. Does everyone know why the choices we are making make sense as the best choices – for the best growth, the most outstanding performance, and the greatest success?

Each of these 9 questions suggests that it would be valuable to have a set of metrics or guides against which you can monitor your progress. This is where the most effective and successful leaders use high quality processes that can move people, teams, and organizations in the best ways possible. The decisions that flow from an outstanding process will more effectively empower, uplift, clarify, focus, and drive individuals and organizations to perform at their best. They will easily out-perform competitors. Even more significantly, these decisions provide a basis for everyone to make and own the most important steps necessary for accelerating valuable results and meaningful success.

I named this structure the Strategic Alignment Process™. The Strategic Alignment Process™ enhances the capability of the smartest and best leaders – and their teams and organizations – to always be equipped to simply and clearly answer these questions:

✧ What are our most important and valuable results – this week, month, quarter, or year?

✧ Why are these the best choices of what is most important?

✧ (Only once you have answered these two questions you are then ready to address:) How can we best achieve these results?

Every smart, successful, and effective leader is always ready to address questions of what really matters most, and why those are the best choices – before they dive into strategies.

The impatient, unprepared, moving-fast-in-too-many-directions leader just constantly shoots initiatives onto his team or organization. This causes what I call the *"strategy du jour" effect* – which is one of the main reasons why people are resistant to change and so disengaged. When every day brings another new set of priorities, why bother engaging with or dealing with the changes required by them, as people know the next day will demand something else again?

Clarity and consistency of focus on what really matters are critical. You engage and motivate your people to drive for those meaningful outcomes when you can validate in intelligent and compelling ways why a certain decision deserves to have a high priority. The **why** a choice matters is the most compelling and engaging factor for getting your people focused.

Would you like to validate this premise about the importance of the **why** in a 2-minute exercise you can try out with any of your teams? Get a group together and ask them to participate in this exercise with you. Ask them to raise their hand as high as they can. Once everyone has their hand up, immediately ask them to raise their hands higher.

What happens every time I have ever done this exercise? The hands go up higher on the second request – even though you asked for them to be raised as high as they can the first time. On the first request, they gave you some compliance with what you asked for.

However, you did not get full commitment and performance from any of your people, as evidenced by what happened with your second request.

What is going on? The simple, yet very important-to-understand answer is that **no one will fully commit to a request or an action until they know** *why* **you are asking them to do something.** This plays out every day on executive teams, in the "trenches," and throughout organizations. High quality leaders always carefully explain why they are making the requests and demands that they make. Poor leaders focus on what they want done, without explanation as to why it matters and makes sense. The difference in engagement, commitment, performance and results is immense!

THE POWER OF PROCESS FOR PERFORMANCE IMPROVEMENT

What typically happens for leadership teams is decision-making by one of these methods:

- ⬦ Autocratic delivery of priorities and to-do's from on-high – they come from that senior executive who likes to dictate what they want to happen
- ⬦ An urgent frenzy of activity as issues become emergencies – that often has the feel of an ocean riptide, the undertow that pulls you out to sea regardless of how much you resist
- ⬦ A "death-march" of decision-making – the forced exercise in group dynamics that seems to get hijacked by the loudest or most persistent person until everyone gives up and agrees so they can get out of the room
- ⬦ A lot of time discussing issues and decisions – only to find everyone has their own interpretation of what you thought the agreed upon decisions were

I urge a very different way to approach leadership team decision-making. **The best possible decision-making results demand 2 critical factors:**

- ✧ Clarity about the most important outcomes – _and_
- ✧ Quality of process that produces this clarity about the most important outcomes

The Strategic Alignment Process™ addresses these typical decision-making deficiencies in its very design, function, and structure. Some of its' core operational principles include:

- ✧ Everyone participates in every decision in a constructive, engaging way – giving every participant a bigger stake in honest and candid contribution
- ✧ Every possible idea is put on the table before deciding which ones to deal with – which ensures attention is not hijacked by low priority items while the important issues get ignored or missed
- ✧ Having clear priorities in the decision-making process that builds a unified foundation that gets stronger and stronger as it keeps being tested and refined
- ✧ The "distillation of best thinking process" produces the fastest, strongest, most collaborative way to elegantly distill down the best decision-making criteria

You can avoid the worst outcomes most meetings produce by having: a strong and reliable process that can be replicated; that is reliable and relatively simple to facilitate; that produces results; and leaves everyone in alignment.

More importantly, **people leave a Strategic Alignment Process™ meeting energized, excited, inspired, clear, focused, and able to communicate the what, why, and how of their priorities.** They have a strong sense of connection and respect for their colleagues and team members because of the Strategic Alignment Process™ way of processing decisions. Most importantly, they have a strong basis for making timely and appropriate decisions, fully aligned with the organizational priorities – because they are based upon the clarity produced by the Strategic Alignment Process™.

Leaderships starts with a highly successful decision-making process. The high-quality decisions that flow from that process are what accelerate and elevate leadership performance and results.

That is what the best and most successful leaders have and use – a powerfully productive process for decision-making that produces profound alignment and results for their organizations.

The Strategic Alignment Process™ builds a structure where the key elements of leadership decision-making are simple to establish and communicate. The following chapters spell out the components of the Strategic Alignment Process™, then show how those elements integrate and synergize to provide this impact that every great leader has.

CHAPTER 4

SUCCESS IN SETTING UP YOUR DECISION-MAKING PROCESS

"It is in your moments of decision that your destiny is shaped."
Tony Robbins

Originally known as Pareto's Law, everyone has heard of the 80-20 rule: 80% of your results come from 20% of your clients, actions, products, and so forth. But here's my new 80-20 rule:

✧ 80% of success is common sense. Less than 20% of the people are using it

The art and science of decision-making has profound, yet simple and common-sense principles that guide it. What is most amazing is that so few people have learned, use, or understand the process for rapid, high-quality decision-making. This is especially true when it comes to group decision-making. Are you ready to continue the crusade to make common-sense principles the drivers of outstanding success?

THE CONTEXT FOR THE STRATEGIC ALIGNMENT PROCESS™

Fundamentally, the most important rationale for the Strategic Alignment Process™ is **the need to produce better results faster.** Every smart team and organization needs to be making that happen. However, almost all struggle to find a consistent process to do just that.

The best first step to better results faster is ensuring that your leadership team's decision-making process is sound, solid, and successful. Here is where the trouble begins for almost every organization. Remember the 3-question test for strategic alignment in the first chapter? With most typical, standard, strategic planning or decision-making sessions, reliable agreement and alignment around top priorities are rare. Neither is there agreement around why the top priorities really are the most important ones. How can you ever expect efficient and effective action in a truly meaningful direction under these conditions?

Everything must start with a clear agreement about <u>what the most important, highest priority results</u> must be. These must then always be validated by a *clear and compelling explanation of <u>why these are the best choices</u>* of what is most important. Then, and only then, are you ready to move to defining **how to achieve these priority results.** Your decision-making process must deliver these simply, effectively, and efficiently.

What is your process to do this?

If you did not do it earlier, test your own leadership team's alignment with the 3-question test. As you saw in Chapter 1, simply collect each of your senior team members' answers one at a time and then compare the collective results. Just ask for answers to these questions:

   ✧ What is our organization's 3-year Vision?
   ✧ What is our organization's Mission?
   ✧ What are our organization's top 3 strategic objectives this year?

The most sobering test of all is doing this 3-question test right after your typical strategic planning session! See how much coherent, cohesive, and comprehensive agreement on the organization's Vision, Mission, and top strategic objectives you really have!

If your traditional strategic planning process is like most organizations, it is a long, drawn out, often painful slog through multiple days of horse-trading to come up with a barely agreeable action plan to achieve some made-up Goals. **Top professionals will tell you that most strategic planning sessions are neither strategic nor good planning** (but that is another issue to deal with – we are here to transcend that problem).

The Strategic Alignment Process™ guarantees (yes, guarantees!) that your team emerges from an inspiring, energizing, and clarifying session with overwhelming consensus and agreement on the most critical factors for great decision-making:

- ✧ The compelling and engaging **Vision** for the company
- ✧ The **Identity** that builds the ultimate coherence about who we are
- ✧ The **Purpose** that clarifies the compelling **why** the organization exists
- ✧ The **Values** that guide the organization's thinking, evaluating, and decision-making
- ✧ The focusing and fortifying **Mission** for the company that provides the rationale for why we do what we do
- ✧ The key measurements and benchmarks for progress and success for the company – also known as the top strategic **Goals**

The process that underlies clarifying these is the start of accelerating your organization's success: taking your leadership through a profoundly powerful and empowering process that **gets everyone focused, on the same page, and committed to producing what really matters.** As simple as this sounds, and as critically important as it is to accomplish, this is way too rare a result of most typical planning sessions.

Nothing will move your team and organization better, faster, and sooner than starting with these core decisions, made together, collectively owned, and done in an engaging and uplifting way. These are the basis of the Strategic Alignment Process™.

These foundational decisions open the gates to making quick, quality decisions as to the best Strategies and Tactics needed to achieve your Goals and fulfilling your Vision and Mission. **When you** agree on what really matters most – and can validate those decisions by explaining why they are the best choices – it becomes infinitely easier to engage the rest of the organization in effective and productive execution. This is the more effective, efficient, and engaging opposite of what too many leaders and organization end up doing – telling their people, "Just do this."

Note the differences in how you and your people would respond to these 2 different approaches:

⬧ Sharing a compelling Vision and Mission that explains why the most critical Goals are meaningful and important – or

⬧ Hoping your people accept your directives to focus on a set of Goals or Strategies they don't fully understand

This is the difference between aligning, accelerating, and activating your people's highest and best engagement and dragging them in some direction they just acquiesce to because you are the boss.

Providing clarity about what really matters most – and why it matters – is far more empowering for many reasons. Prime among them is that your managers and front-line people now engage with greater clarity and understanding about what results that the organization aspires to – versus just hearing about tactics you want them to use.

Two key axioms of success that guide the thinking and practices of Strategic Alignment are:

⬧ Results are worth far more than any Strategy, process, or set of actions

⬧ Connecting people to a meaningful sense of Purpose – the "why they are there" – is far more compelling and engaging than even results

Understanding these two principles, you would always:

⬧ Start with clear results to ensure that your people are clear, focused on, and committed to reaching the goal line

✧ Validate why these are the best possible choices and measurements of accomplishment for a fulfilling and compelling Purpose, Mission and Vision

Generating these critical clarifications well (more about that coming up) are essential for an alignment process that works. What is most often missing is articulating the **why** – done in powerfully engaging ways that connects your team and people to the **what** that needs to be accomplished.

By activating the power of Purpose you light the human rocket fuel that engages the best in and from your people. You get them connected to the reasons why they are there and why doing their job really matters. Connecting to the **why** of their work is far more compelling, engaging, motivating, and activating than "what you want them to achieve" (Goals) and the "how to get things done" (Strategies).

THE DECISION-MAKING PROCESS PRINCIPLES AND STRUCTURE

You have been reading about the key elements of decision-making and decision-making process. What is remarkable to understand is that there are only a few drivers of decision-making effectiveness. The challenge for most leaders is that they have not mastered decision-making that:

✧ Distinguishes the value and proper usage of each of these key elements

✧ Utilizes an effective process to integrate and align these elements well

✧ Facilitates their team's agreement on the "What, Why, and How" decisions

✧ Produces coherent, congruent, consistent, clarity and communication that influences and focuses their people for optimal results

Below is a map of the structure and process that defines powerful decision-making. Utilizing these principles appropriately in a coherent process produces a profound increase in the speed, clarity, focus and impact of your decision-making.

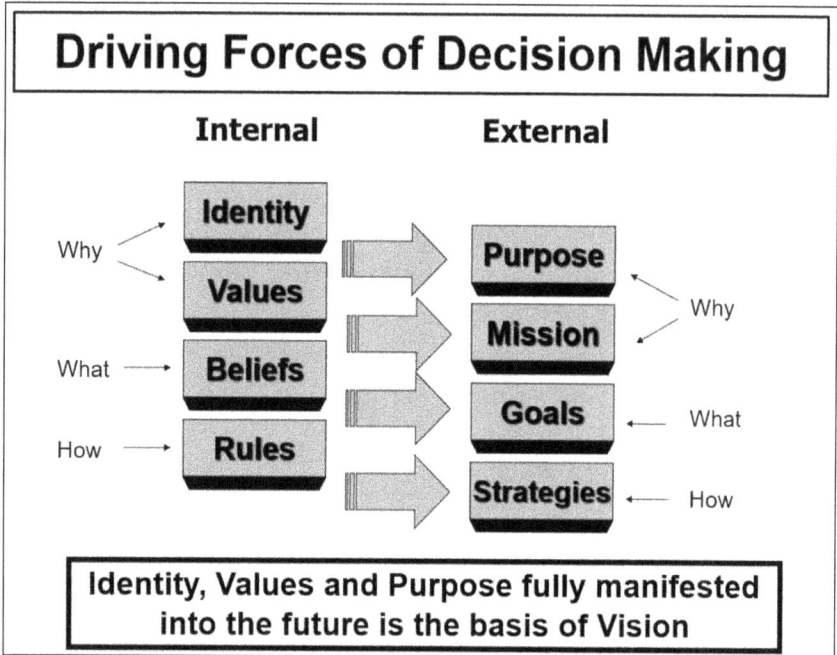

Driving Forces of Decision Making

Internal   **External**

Identity

Why

Values   **Purpose**

Why

Mission

What   **Beliefs**

Goals   What

How   **Rules**

Strategies   How

Identity, Values and Purpose fully manifested into the future is the basis of Vision

What you are looking at is how each of these elements, principles, and drivers relate to each other, and fit in the hierarchy of decision-making process. Every single one of these elements is powerful, important, and must be present and clearly articulated for optimal results. The "internal" elements on the left side of this chart are the starting point and most important drivers of the decisions on the right side. The decisions that they powerfully influence are noted by what the arrows containing the word "Drive" point to.

⬧ Identity and Values influence Purpose
⬧ Identity, Values, and Purpose manifested in the future is the basis for Vision

⟡ Values and Empowering Beliefs influence Mission, in alignment with Purpose and Vision
⟡ Beliefs and Rules influence Goals, in alignment with Mission, Vision, and Purpose
⟡ Rules influence Strategies, in alignment with Goals, Mission, Vision, and Purpose

The hierarchy of decisions is also important to understand. The most powerful principles are at the top of each side of the chart. When these most powerful principles are clear and well-utilized, they drive better and faster decision-making as you work down each element below it. This is the essence of why process matters.

The importance and impact of each of these elements, as well as the inter-relationship between them is what the rest of this book is about.

Rest assured that these basic elements open the door to the decision-making process and decisions that promise to elevate and accelerate your leadership impact and results.

DECISION-MAKING AND ENGAGEMENT AT WORK

As is too often noted in social research – more than 70% of employees are disengaged at work. The costs to productivity, profitability, fulfillment, and results for all parties are enormous. Time and time again studies have shown what people want most is a sense of purpose and meaning in their work. A compelling sense of purpose and values that resonate are among the best, fastest, and most powerful ways to give people what they so strongly want.

That is how you bring out their best ownership, initiative, and sense of responsibility to achieve important and meaningful results. Engagement and taking responsibility are 2 of the qualities leaders always say they want more of from their team members.

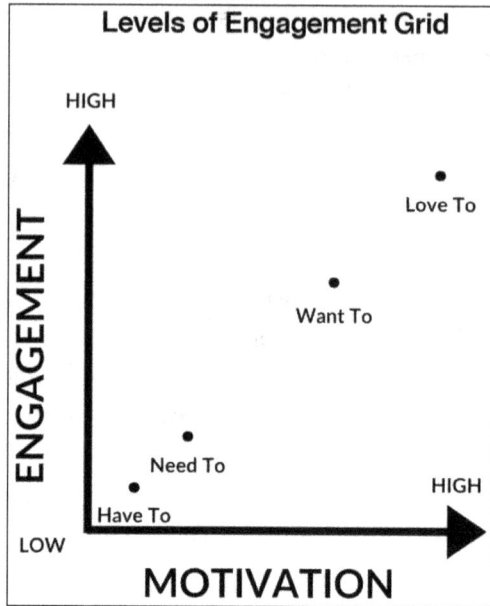

Levels of Engagement Grid

As you can see from this graphic, the most engaging levels that moti-vate people are what they want and love. What people most want in a business context (as well as a personal one) is a sense of purpose, connected with a strong sense of identity and congruence with what they value most. Add in a vision that inspires them, and you have what the highest performing people and organizations have and thrive on.

When the purpose of your organization is clear and compelling to your people, they will **want** to achieve the goals and execute on the strategies. Their desire for accomplishment and responsibility is stim-ulated by a strong connection to knowing why they are after these objectives. Knowing **why** they are doing something is the best way to engage your people to **want**, and even **love**, to achieve beyond their normal capacity.

When the purpose of your organization is neither clear nor com-pelling, what you hear most often relative to goals and strategies is: "What do I **have to** accomplish and do?" This indicates a lack of ownership, which most often results in your people waiting to be told what they have to do. Not knowing why they are being asked to accomplish a specific goal and implement some specific strategy significantly reduces their level of engagement, responsibility, and passion for directives from above.

At what level of engagement do you most want your people operating? Do they have the clarity of Purpose, Identity, and Values that makes that happen?

Check out your senior team and organization, and consider, on a 1 (low) to 10 (high) scale (of course, you want a 10 on these):

⬦ Is our Purpose, Vision, and Mission engaging, compelling, and motivating for all our people?
⬦ Are our top 3 strategic objectives clear and providing meaningful progress in fulfilling our Mission and Vision?
⬦ Are these providing what people want and love about being a part of who we are?

Only a resounding "yes" is an acceptable answer – if you value having a highly engaged, high performing, high achieving team and organization. Anything less than a 10 means you have work to do generating more compelling clarity that produces better organizational engagement – and the kinds of results you really want from your people. In all likelihood, you have missed or fallen short on one or more of the Strategic Alignment Process™ elements.

ACCELERATING AND ELEVATING YOUR RESULTS

The power of the Strategic Alignment Process™ is that by doing the work of determining the underlying, foundational, "inner" decisions (Identity, Values, Beliefs, and Rules), it makes the other choices of Purpose, Vision, Mission, Goals, and Strategies immensely simpler and easier!

This is the structure that is impeccable, reliable, much more powerful, and faster in generating your most important results. You might ask: does it work in every organization? Yes, it does – and it has delivered these results every time it is implemented.

In fact, facilitation of the Strategic Alignment Process™ comes with an ironclad guarantee. If you do not achieve overwhelming consensus in an energizing and engaging way on your Vision, Values, Mission, and Goals, you pay nothing for your session. Most organizations have struggled through their strategic planning with mostly inadequate results – especially given all the talent in the room.

The Strategic Alignment Process™ comes with clear and compelling outcomes along with a process that guarantees to deliver the desired results.

What could this do to elevating the enthusiasm of your people, the clarity of your decision-making, and the focus on results that delivers the most outstanding success?

The next two sections of the book explain why the process that produces Strategic Alignment works – and how to deliver that result.

When you want to find out more – and get to work massively accelerating your results – contact Steve Lishansky, CEO, at:

✧ 978-369-4525

✧ Info@OptimizeIntl.com

✧ www.OptimizeIntl.com

✧ Schedule a 20-minute, insight-filled call at https://OptimizeCalendar.com

"You cannot make progress without making decisions."

Jim Rohn

SECTION 2

THE SECRETS OF THE STRATEGIC ALIGNMENT PROCESS™

"The beginning is the most important part of the work."
Plato

CHAPTER 5

THE STRATEGIC ALIGNMENT PROCESS – THE INTERNAL ELEMENTS

*"It is our choices, Harry, that show
what we truly are, far more than our abilities."*

Professor Dumbledore in *Harry Potter and the
Chamber of Secrets* by J. K. Rowling

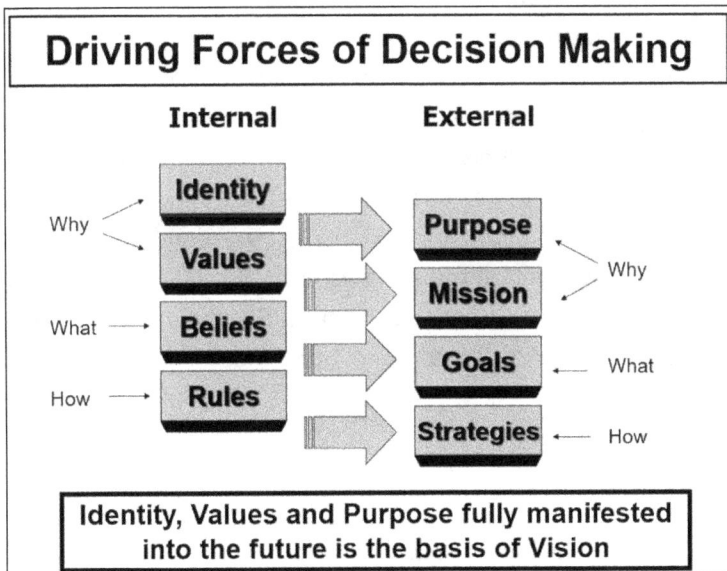

Driving Forces of Decision Making

Internal   **External**

Why

Identity

Values

Purpose

Why

What → Beliefs

Mission

How → Rules

Goals ← What

Strategies ← How

**Identity, Values and Purpose fully manifested
into the future is the basis of Vision**

As you review the 9 core elements above (be sure to include vision in the box at the bottom) and listed out below, you may already notice elements in your decision-making process that are weak, not well formulated, or just plain missing.

The distinctions on the left side, noted as *internal,* reflect what are often called the sub-conscious or neurologically based elements in individuals. In the context of an organization, these are the elements that comprise the culture of your company.

By saying these are internal or neurologically-based means that these already exist and influence your decisions. However, they are rarely thoughtfully chosen or consciously designed. This also means that they are usually not very clear, not often discussed or clarified, and not as effective as you would want for creating the kind of culture you would love to have.

When these internal factors are not clear, well-chosen, reflective of what you aspire to, most of your conscious choices (on the right side of the graphic) are guaranteed to be weaker and less coherent than you want and need. The correlation between the choices of Identity, Values, Beliefs, and Rules and how they are instrumental in clarifying the Purpose, Vision, Mission, Goals, and Strategies is one of the most fundamental and powerful insights contained within the Strategic Alignment Process™.

Fully utilizing these elements and relationships produces a level of speed, impact, and results in decision-making that is dazzlingly effective. When your decision-making is, then organizational congruence, effectiveness, performance, and results to a whole new level of success!

Fully utilizing the elements and how they integrate with and impact each other forms a perfect foundation for effective decisions. These are the decisions that come from a coherent and congruent decision-making process.

OVERVIEW OF THE INTERNAL ELEMENTS

Let's consider each of these elements, including looking at how they work and what they represent. In subsequent chapters you will learn how to facilitate the process that draws out high quality and insightful responses, including integrating all the responses to create the most powerful structure for decision-making.

IDENTITY

The most powerful element of human decision-making is your Identity. The simplest way to understand Identity is that it is what you believe you are in each dimension of your life. People will do more to act congruently with their Identity than anything else. Whether the Identity you believe you are is about your gender, nationality, religion, relationship, political affiliation, title in an organization, or any of the other way in which we identify who we are, our connection to Identity is supremely powerful. Even though they are subconscious or loaded in our nervous system, these Identities are the powerful foundations of how we see ourselves, hold our personal congruence, and make our decisions.

A remarkable fact of life is that the Identity of most has not been consciously chosen. In the context of organizational Identity, the closest most come to articulating their Identities is in the form of marketing phrases and statements rarely manifest the power of Identity. Instead, they are Beliefs about how to be perceived. A strong Identity statement, consciously chosen to reflect who you really are, empowers deep congruence, whether we are talking about an individual or an organization.

Compare these two different approaches to Identity. "We are the most creative and innovative team," versus reframing this statement into: "We are the source of innovation and creativity." That simple 'reframing' dramatically ups the level of clarity, engagement and passion.

For another example, we could look at 3 roles that I have, as an:

◇ Executive coach
◇ Strategic planning facilitator
◇ Professional speaker on leadership

While these are all worthy and noble, note how they pale in comparison to the Identities that drive my professional work:

⋄ I am the healer of corporate blindness
⋄ I am the source for decision-making insight and impact
⋄ I am the powerful partner in elevating and accelerating clients' results

Which of these engage and inspire you more – the roles or identities? Who would you rather work with knowing only the roles or Identities that you see here?

You will find more about how to deeply engage your professional and organizational Identity and other elements as you proceed through this book.

VALUES

I call Values the most accessible level of transformation. What you and your organization determine to be your most important, highest priority Values to uphold and base your decision-making on refines all your thinking rapidly, clearly, and profoundly.

Everyone defines whether they are doing well or not to a large degree based upon how congruent they are with their Values. However, for the vast majority of people, their Values are only a vague notion or feeling. How they feel tells them that they are operating according to their Values or not. The reason it is at best a vague notion or feeling is that most people could not tell you clearly what they value most. More significantly, very few people or organizations can tell you the priority ranking of their Values.

Test this out with yourself and your people. At an appropriate moment, ask your top individuals and then your team: "What are your top 4 Values, in priority order?" You will be met initially by silence. That is followed by a response that is pretty random. Do this yourself and see how clear your own Values are.

When you and your colleagues come up with your Values, you can bet that many of these are a sub-set that I call "Means Values." Means Values are **actions** or **things** that are a "means" of the actual and of being

What people really most value are what I call "Ends Values." Ends Values are those and states of being that we as humans most prize. There is a quantum difference between Means Values – which are actions or things – and Ends Value – those most important and meaningful feelings we want to experience in our life as keys to fulfillment.

Ends Values tend to be prized across cultures and by humanity in general. Here are a few examples of common Ends Values that you will find treasured across virtually all cultures:

- ✧ Connection
- ✧ Contribution
- ✧ Courage
- ✧ Creativity
- ✧ Freedom
- ✧ Growth
- ✧ Integrity
- ✧ Joy
- ✧ Love
- ✧ Passion
- ✧ Recognition
- ✧ Respect
- ✧ Security
- ✧ Success
- ✧ Vitality

However, too often people are focused on the means to these ends, rather than the Ends Value feelings they really most want. For example, your people might be saying they want a raise, a promotion, a better title, more money, a transfer, more travel, less travel, more time with friends and family, time off, a new car, a better house, new clothes, and on and on. When you look at this list, **these are all things** or actions. They are only the means to what someone really wants to feel.

When you ask most people what is most important about more money, the most common Ends Values that show up are: freedom or security or recognition or all of these. These are the feelings that they really want to feel, which they believe will come from having certain things, like a raise or more money. Try it out.

One of the earliest confirmations of this principle came years ago when we discussed the difference between means and ends Values with a client. Pounding his fist on the table, his enthusiasm getting him jumping out of his chair, this executive exclaimed: "I just had this happen last month!"

One of his most valuable people came to him and said he was leaving unless he got significantly more money. In an economically tight time, the boss was still able to arrange to get this high performer a $25,000 raise. Within a month of receiving what was a large raise in this organization, this valued employee gave his notice and left.

In the exit interview, especially in light of having just received this large raise, his answer to why he was leaving after getting what he asked for was: "I have been asking for more recognition, responsibility, and growth opportunities for over a year. Frustrated that it was not happening fast enough, I finally said 'Just give me more money, because I deserve it."

He went to a new company that gave him a more significant role and title and slightly less money. However, the company also promised him continued growth opportunities, recognition, and reward. Failing to see that the money was just a *means* to even more important *ends* the recognition, responsibility, and growth that the person really wanted most cost the first company dearly.

When someone is asking for a thing or action which is always a means to an end it is valuable to find out what Ends Values they are seeking. That can be as simple as asking "What is most important about "x" (the thing or action? Most , this question ensures the likelihood of providing what is truly desired and valued.

When you ask most people what is most important about time off, or more time with friends and family, the most common Ends

Values that come up are: love or connection or joy or all of these. Again, these are the really important feelings that they want to feel, which they believe they will feel when they have more time or more time with friends and family. Test this out for yourself that what people most often are asking for is really only the thing they think will give them what they really long for and most want.

In the context of Strategic Alignment, having clarity of Values for your team and organization provides a strong, focused, compelling foundation for knowing you have the right people focused on the right things.

Below are Values defined by 10 different client groups, and listed in the priority order they chose. Just reading these sets of Values begin to imagine the priorities, they would attract:

◈ Committed, Cooperative, Focused, Adaptable, Respected
◈ Trusted, Connected, Contributing, Learning and Growing
◈ Contributing, Connected, Courageous, Impactful, Generous
◈ Innovative, Collaborative, Passionate, Engaged, Contributing
◈ Passionate, Trusting, Collaborative, Flexible, Open, Creative
◈ Impactful, Learning and Growing, Compassionate, Collaborative
◈ Integrity, Focused, Collaborative, Adaptable, Driven
◈ Success, Learning and Growing, Integrity, Fun, Passion
◈ Excellence, Integrity, Adaptable, Innovative, Respected
◈ Clarity, Consistency, Honesty, Collaborative, Joy

As you review these Values from different organizations, you can easily get a picture what kind of organization each is. You can also get an idea about what kind of people would be attracted to cultures with Values like these. Although a few of the same Values appear on multiple lists, the order of priority order and other Values listed provide significant differentiation .

For instance, valuing performance over loyalty produces a very different organization and culture than valuing loyalty over performance. This question of whether to value performance or loyalty more highly is one of those choices that often stymies organizations from moving forward – because they don't have a clear priority choice between these 2 Values. What we claim as our Values provides a container or framework for our thinking and decision-making.

The strongest cultures are built on a platform of clear and congruent Values, supported by well aligned Beliefs and Rules that people understand and buy into. It is very hard to buy into Values, Beliefs, or Rules that are not clearly spelled out.

EMPOWERING BELIEFS

One of my favorite definitions of a Belief is that it is an idea or feeling that we no longer question. Beliefs reflect what we think is real and or possible in the world. Beliefs in many ways are the glasses through which we see, experience, and judge our experiences.

For example, those who tend to believe things are good and usually turn out well are known as optimists. They make very different decisions in the same situations than pessimists – the people who believe things will usually turn out poorly. Confronting the exact same scenario, optimists and pessimists will believe in the likelihood of very different outcomes. Clearly their choices are based more on how they look at the actual facts of the situation.

Beliefs are enormously powerful. They are the backbone of religion, for instance. The beliefs you hold determine how you see the world. What you believe happens after death influences your decisions and behaviors in the present– even without evidence. Yet those Beliefs are enormously influential in your decisions.

People also carry many , and conflicting Beliefs at the same time. Many of our great societal Beliefs – the things our parents and teachers may have taught us – are very much in conflict. Which you choose to follow depends upon what you believe is really the more compelling choice. Here are some examples of popular, yet opposing, Beliefs:

- ✧ He who hesitates is lost, *versus* Look before you leap
- ✧ Strike while the iron is hot, *versus* Rome was not built in a day
- ✧ Speak up, *versus* Silence is golden

- ✧ A stitch in time saves nine, *versus* A watched pot never boils
- ✧ The early bird catches the worm, *versus* Who laughs last laughs best

I could certainly cite many more, some of which you might be holding right now. Often the "push-pull" of decision-making at the level of Beliefs happens when your opposing ones show up. This obviously makes your choosing challenging. When you are making decisions at the level of Beliefs, most often people make those decisions based upon a strong, held belief about how something is. The challenging aspect about decision-making at this level is that people are often strongly impelled to defend their choices. They do that despite – regardless of facts.

Unless you know you are stuck on making a belief-driven decision, it is often hard to let go of highly biased certainty. When you have strongly held Beliefs, people usually make up Rules to ensure that their Beliefs are sustained and supported.

RULES

I define Rules as the actions that must be followed in order to experience an important Value. That is, these are the determiners of the actions needed in order to "win at the game of our Values" Whether those are the Values that we hold as important in our personal professional, or worlds, we must follow these very specific Rules in order to get and feel what we want most.

Most of us have played Monopoly or chess or blackjack at some time in our lives. Each of these games has very specific Rules about what you can and cannot do in order to win. You must make each decision and choose each action in accordance with the Rules of what is acceptable. Only by following the Rules can you play the game.

The Rules for fulfilling our Values are similarly set up. You must have Rules to fulfill and experience what you Value. What is most important to understand is that these Rules are buried in our nervous systems, determining whether or not we get to feel the Values that we most want to experience. However, most people have not consciously developed Rules that work well for them in the context of what they Value most. Instead, their experiences are subject to whatever Rules they may have unconsciously or accidentally chosen, often at an early age, without consideration for the consequences of their choices.

Rules in organizations are disconnected in the same way, and fail to ensure that their Values are fulfilled. Furthermore, Rules drive the lowest level of compliance. That is, if you require following Rules in order to keep people focused on what is most important, you will see a very low level of engagement. These compliance-oriented Rules are often highly directive or recriminative, and many times also reference penalties for non-compliance. These are often stated as negatives, and define what cannot or should not be done. You would find specific actions included in statements stated as "you must..." or "you have to..." or "if you do... then you will be..."

A highly and dependable team is driven by their Values, Mission, and most important objectives. These are the drivers that inspire to step up and e on more responsibility than you might even ask for or expect. Rules-driven people simply do what they are told, without offering up any more than what is required.

Rules are important but they are most effective when consciously chosen in the context of well-defined Values and empowering Beliefs. Used in this way they are clarifiers of what needs to be done for attaining what is most important and worthwhile – their Values results. Rules used any other way are instruments of control and restriction, which diminishes their value in elevating an organization.

To reiterate, **Rules are meaningful in the service of clarifying what it takes to fulfill the Values that matter most.** That is their highest and best use. Used any other way, they result in a lower level of functioning, often driven by a desire to limit and control people or situations. That is the very antithesis of an empowered, growth-oriented, responsible team and organization.

CHAPTER 6

STRATEGIC ALIGNMENT PROCESS™ – THE EXTERNAL ELEMENTS

"Leadership is the capacity to translate vision into reality."
Warren Bennis

Driving Forces of Decision Making

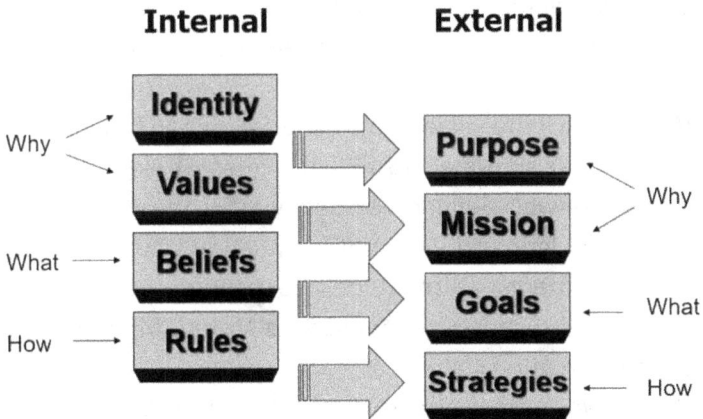

Internal	External

Internal

Identity

Why

Values

What → Beliefs

How → Rules

External

Purpose

Mission ← Why

Goals ← What

Strategies ← How

Identity, Values and Purpose fully manifested into the future is the basis of Vision

What is quite remarkable about these "external elements" is that, unlike the "internal elements," these are elements that must be chosen. They are decisions that must be made. The internal elements already exist as unconscious drivers in an individual's nervous system and an organization's culture. What the internal elements often suffer from is that rarely are they:

✧ Clear
✧ Well thought out
✧ Consciously considered
✧ Communicated effectively

If the internal elements are weak or unclear, then their ability to be a foundation for making a positive impact on the decisions about the external elements is also going to be weak. This is another of the critical outcomes that the Strategic Alignment Process™ transforms.

OVERVIEW OF THE EXTERNAL ELEMENTS

All of these external elements require choices, and do not exist until someone makes a decision. What these external elements often suffer from is:

1. Most or all of these elements especially when lacking the solid basis of decision-making that the internal elements provide are neither well-defined nor clearly articulated
2. They lack clear and useful differentiation between these different elements as most people cannot make useful and meaningful distinctions between a Vision, Mission, Goal, or Strategy
3. These two factors above combine to further constraint the usefulness of these external elements especially limiting their capacity to work together as a well-integrated, decision-making process

The key to success with empowering these critical elements that are the of Purpose, Mission, Vision, Goals, and Strategies is to have done the work of defining the internal elements well. Look closely at the Driving Forces of the Decision-Making graphic. Notice how the arrows are connected and what they influence:

✧ Identity and Values as drivers of Purpose

✧ Identity, Values, and Purpose as drivers of Vision

✧ Values and Beliefs as drivers of Mission, in alignment with Purpose and Vision

✧ Beliefs and Rules as drivers of Goals, in alignment with Vision and Mission

✧ Rules as drivers of Strategies, in alignment with Vision, Mission, and Goals

To reiterate – **the important point about these external elements and choices is that in addition to being driven by the corresponding internal elements, they need to be in alignment with the external element above it.** That is, Mission needs to be in the service of and in alignment with the Purpose and Vision. The Goals need to be in the service of and alignment with the Mission. The Strategies need to be in the service of and alignment with the Goals.

Of course, applying my new "80/20 "would make these points seem like good, basic, common sense.

✧ **The Purpose of Strategies is to define how best to achieve your Goals**

✧ **The Purpose of Goals is to define what are the benchmarks or measurements of success in fulfilling your Mission and Vision**

✧ **The Purpose of Mission is to define why you make the choices and decisions about who to be and what to do in fulfilling your Vision**

Most leaders and most organizations do not do the critically important foundation building that drives the best and most effective choices of Vision, Mission, Goals, and Strategies. They don't clearly articulate the organizational Identity, Values, Beliefs, and Rules. Without these elements being clearly defined, it is extremely difficult to develop a clear, coherent, congruent consensus around Vision, Mission, Goals, and Strategies.

This failure leads to making up Goals that cannot be validated with good reasons as to why they matter. That leads to extended battles over Strategies.

The smooth alignment of each element in relationship to the other elements is what gives you certainty that your Strategic Alignment Process™ structure does indeed make sense. The Strategic Alignment of your Vision, Mission, Goals, and Strategies provides an integrated clarity about:

◈ What is really most important to focus on which is articulated by your Goals

◈ Why your Goals are the best choices of what to focus on and measure success and progress by which is articulated by your Vision and Mission

◈ How you will achieve your Goals which are articulated by your Strategies

How many companies have a Vision and Mission that makes sense, organizes their decision-making, and engages their people and clients with enthusiasm and commitment? Not enough. **Correcting this major cause of lack of clarity and engagement is one of my most important Goals.**

This is the problem with doing traditional, pedestrian strategic planning. We all recognize that this needs to be done, but it doesn't seem to enhance the clarity, focus, and alignment among our leaders and teams! What happens with poor planning is that people in the meeting accept poorly articulated statements of whichever of these distinctions of Vision, Mission, Goals, and Strategies they think they might need.

Planning team members don't even know to look for and demand all 4 of these critical decision-making factors – Vision, Mission, Goals, and Strategies – much less a clear alignment among all 4. They willingly acquiesce to almost anything that sounds decent because their process is so convoluted, confusing, and difficult. Getting it over with takes precedence over having clarity of focus that delivers impact, value, and meaningful results for their organization.

The Strategic Alignment Process™ is as energizing and thoroughly enjoyable as it is powerful and capable of immense impact. That pretty much defines the opposite of most strategic planning, especially as it is typically practiced. Ask any group of executives whether they would like to review their Vision and Mission and participate in a strategic planning process. You know what a typical response looks like – eye rolls, head shakes, requests for time off to visit the dentist instead.

It is easy to see why this is enormously sad and detrimental to driving growth, improving results, and building engagement. Most organizations and leaders are at a point where the powerful and important foundations for decision-making that every organization should prize is relegated to either an afterthought or a death march type of meeting.

The Strategic Alignment Process™ provides a solution that most leaders, teams, and organizations need. That is the ability to make powerfully important decisions in a way that focuses an organization for faster, better, and more effective decision-making by all.

This is where leadership starts. This is where developing your people and organization start. This is where exceptional impact and results begins.

When you are ready to significantly upgrade you and your team's focus and results, start by looking at the external elements and how they work in conjunction with the internal elements you have already been introduced to.

PURPOSE

Your Purpose is the ultimate reason why your organization exists. If you randomly ask most executives why your organization exists, you are most likely going to get a blank stare or a mushy, rambling answer. However, harnessing the power of Purpose is one of the most potent practices for engaging your people at a profoundly energizing level.

What is especially important to note is that clarifying Purpose is both simple and fast once you have built the foundation of Identity and Values. When you want to articulate why your organization exists, it must be built upon and integrated with the answers to the questions of who you are and what really matters most. This is exactly what your Identity and Values establishes.

At the confluence of these "internal" distinctions lies the almost obvious decision about why your organization exists. Without clarity about who you are and what really matters already having been defined, quantifying your Purpose is like shooting in the dark. You might hit something, but it is extremely hard to say with compelling confidence that you have identified why you exist. This is why most Purpose exercises are random explorations They wander around seeking consensus, which all too often is of the lowest common denominator type. These kind of Purpose exercises lack the essential foundations that give rise to a solid and satisfying decision.

VISION

Many of the better thinkers and transformation agents today are rightfully extolling the power of Purpose. However, when you unite Purpose with the power of Identity and Values, these collectively produce the profound captivation that makes a compelling Vision the most profound statement of all.

Think about it. What could be more compelling than engaging with the 3 most powerful forces of humanity, and imagining what is possible when fully manifesting them in the future? That is how you create the picture called your Vision. Your Vision builds on manifesting your answers to the 3 most powerful and ancient philosophical questions mankind has been asking since the beginning of time:

1. Who am I?
2. Why am I here?
3. What really matters?

By our definition, **your Vision is what you, your team, and your organization will see as the future when you have fully manifested your Identity, Values, and Purpose.**

Your Vision is an exceptionally powerful statement about what you will see in the future. That could be 1 year, 3 years, 5 years, or whatever point in the future you choose. In the Strategic Alignment Process™, Vision comes out of integrating your Identity, Values, and Purpose in the future. It encapsulate the power of each of these elements into a collective whole that is even more powerful than the parts. When Vision is designed and done well, the articulation represents the impact of these 3 most powerful forces of decision-making: your Identity, Purpose, and Values. What could be more powerful, illuminating, and engaging to your team, people, and organization?

The Strategic Alignment Process™ elegantly and effectively facilitates the answers to these 3 profound questions for your organization. Defining these 3 elements well gives you and your people this platform to stand on to create a future you can articulate that is worth having. As important, it is engaging and compelling to start working for right now, in the present. As great leaders and philosophers have said: "If you don't create your own future, someone else will."

Picturing a Vision built on fully manifesting your Identity, Purpose, and Values is the most grounded yet inspiring process for creating that future. Done well, it is built on what will fuel inspiration, engagement, and focus the most. Without applying the principles of the Strategic Alignment Process™ you are once again left wandering in the dark trying to cook up something but without the recipe and ingredients that make it work.

MISSION

Your Purpose and Vision create the global perspective and focus on why you exist and what that existence could look like when fully and brilliantly manifested in the future. Your Mission refines your focus as to why your choices matter now. Missions define and contain the clearest reasons you and your organization make the choices that you do. If your Purpose is the 360-degree reason why you exist, then your Mission is in many respects the 90-degree quadrant of focus you use to define the "why you are making the decisions you do."

There are no two elements in the Strategic Alignment Process™ decision-making matrix more alike than Purpose and Mission. They must be fully aligned, supportive of each other. Still, they are different. Each of them, while similar, requires different processing. They utilize different underlying, "internal" elements to create a solid platform.

Where Purpose is built on the foundation of Identity and Values, Mission is built on the basis of Values and Beliefs. Mission must also be in alignment with and serve Purpose and Vision. Purpose, Mission and Vision are key answers to the question, "Why are we here and doing what we are doing?"

What makes Mission so important is that it provides a focal point against which you can validate your choices. When are you faced with a decision you can always ask: "Is this congruent with and supportive of fulfilling on our Mission?" You can further validate your Mission by asking: "When we accomplish our Mission, does that move us closer to fulfilling our Purpose and Vision?"

These questions test the mutual alignment, strength, and congruence that ensure your focus is clear enough to make meaningful and productive decisions.

While your Purpose articulates the biggest, broadest, and most engaging **why** you and your organization exist, it is balanced by your Mission, the criteria why what you are and what you do matters. While Purpose makes you and your people feel good about why your organization matters, your Mission gives more focus to what matters in making decisions.

If Purpose is your 360-degree reason why you exist and matter, Mission reflects a more specific quadrant of focus and importance. I call that the 90-degree segment that most effectively focuses everyone on both what matters most as well as why that is so.

Here are some examples of Purposes and Missions that demonstrate these differences:

✧ **Purpose:** Be the driver of profitable customer acquisition and growth – and the economic engine of our business communities
✧ **Mission:** Be the division of growth that foresees and meets the needs of our customers, colleagues, and community now and for the future

✧ **Purpose:** Transform access to the best medical expertise globally and provide people the tools and confidence to achieve their best possible health
✧ **Mission:** Reimagine healthcare by aligning world-class clinical expertise with digital technology to make it easier to get the best healthcare

✧ **Purpose:** Leave a tangible legacy for our communities, company, and people
✧ **Mission:** Solve the complex and valuable problems that make our environment better

✧ **Purpose:** Fulfill unmet needs in healing and wellness
✧ **Mission:** Generate innovative healing modalities and educate providers and clients in outcome driven, personalized wellness

✧ **Purpose:** Distill, deliver and inspire the world's best business thinking
✧ **Mission:** Build the world's most respected library of actionable business insight that engages and energizes business audiences

✧ **Purpose:** Build an enduring company that maximizes sustainability and efficiency across global supply chains
✧ **Mission:** Empowering businesses in the global food system to maximize sustainability and efficiency (*note their initial mission focus on one aspect of the global supply chain*)

As you challenge your decision-making to ensure it effectively serves your Mission, you can also ask if that Mission will serve your Purpose and support the manifestation of your Vision. This is the art of ensuring each element is strong in its own right, as well as integrated and aligned into a decision-making structure that makes sense and works!

GOALS

Defining Goals a little differently than most people do provides a clearer and better way to gauge if they are really serving their intended Purpose. When you position your Goals as **the measurements of accomplishment of your Mission and Vision**, it makes it clear how you can validate them. Each Goal should be a strong stepping-stone that gets you closer to fulfilling your Mission. As just noted in the previous section, your Mission must be effective for fulfilling your Purpose and Vision.

In the context of the meta-questions that these distinctions clarify, Goals move from the realm of "" and the question of "" we are making the choices we are making – as Identity, Purpose, Values, Mission, and Vision do. **Goals move us into the realm of thinking and answering the question of "what is really most important."** Goals provide a way to address such questions as:

⬥ What matters most?

⬥ What needs to be monitored and measured to ensure progress?

⬥ What meaningful benchmarks or accomplishments will move us forward in fulfilling our Mission and Vision?

This is the "what to focus on" in service of the "why we are here" of your organization.

Goals articulate and focus us on what is most important for ensuring progress and success. They are validated by being able to explain why they are the best choices to focus on, as articulated by the Vision and Mission that the Goals serve.

Once the **what** and **why** are clear and coherent, and they have overwhelming consensus among your key leaders and people, you are ready to define how you will accomplish the Goals, which in turn will fulfill your Mission and Vision.

Your Goals, as measurements of accomplishment, need to be quantifiable. Many leaders at first think that must be an absolutely objective measurement. However, regularly gathered and measured subjective opinions can offer you an objective trend (i.e. we are improving versus we are declining). This is particularly useful for important subjective topics such as quality of: leadership, communication, employee engagement, customer satisfaction, and so forth. These are clearly subjective opinions, yet they are important ones Gathering evaluations on topics like these on a regular basis produces an upward or downward trend and useful.

Too often people and leaders do not distinguish clearly between the Goals and the Strategies of their organization. This demarcation between the measurements of accomplishment (Goals) and the set of actions that will keep you moving towards your Goals (Strategies) is important to differentiate.

Having clear Goals tells you what to focus on. Once this is clear and validated your attention and decision-making moves to how to think about what to do. Your Goals, as measurements of accomplishment, when done well, naturally ignite thinking about how to do what it takes to accomplish the most important measurements.

STRATEGIES

Once you have clarity and agreement on your Goals as the most important measurements of accomplishment of your Vision and Mission, it is time to progress in your decision-making to how to achieve these Goals. These decisions about what to do are based on your Strategies. At the most basic level, I call these the "how" you will accomplish your most important Goals.

Strategies are the actions we consider, prioritize, and then act upon to move us forward towards our achievements and accomplishments. My experience is that most organizations are good at doing things. **What is often problematic is when the activities do not add up to accomplishing results that really matter.**

Typically, leaders and teams spend an inordinate amount of time discussing how they will get things done. I say inordinate because, if you were to watch most major organizations, you'll see that they spend more time on Strategies than on Goals, Mission, or Vision. When this imbalance of over-attention and deliberation on Strategies is taking place, it is an immediate indication that, in all likelihood:

⬦ The Goals are not well defined or not really agreed upon

⬦ The Mission is ill-defined or missing altogether

⬦ The Vision is not being used as the "North Star" to guide decision-making

Done well, the Strategies will be clear and well aligned to achieving meaningful Goals, which in turn have direct impact on fulfilling the Mission and Vision. Done well, the entire Strategic Alignment Process™ ends up integrating each of these elements into a coherent decision-making structure.

As noted, the heart of that structure allows you to clearly and simply articulate:

⬦ What is most important

⬦ Why those choices of what is most important are the best choices

⬦ How those most important outcomes will be achieved

What, why and how. These essential decision-making elements are illuminated clearly and incorporated completely into the Strategic Alignment Process™.

CHAPTER 7

CLOSING THE DECISION-MAKING GAPS

*"There is nothing so useless as doing efficiently
That which should not be done at all."*
Peter Drucker

In discussing the specific elements of this decision-making frame-work, part of the immense power of the process comes from ensuring that everyone participates productively, engages fully in the deliberations, and embraces the ownership of the final decisions. The teams that work through the Strategic Alignment Process™ always come to recognize the power of this axiom: **Clarity of outcome and quality of process produces the most outstanding results.** This is valuable and appropriate to every gathering where important results are a necessity

The most significant outcome of the Strategic Alignment Process™ is your team's collectively agreed upon, clearly defined thinking. The Strategic Alignment Process™ delivers the critical decision-making criteria to drive your organization. Accomplishing this in the highest quality way raises the level of engagement and participation, as well as the certainty that what was done will reliably stand the test of time.

The participants in too many strategic planning sessions seem to lose commitment to what was decided within a short time after the sessions are completed. The more collectively generated, and trusted the ownership of the decisions is, the more commitment can be counted on to continue after the session on the part of both the session participants and the people in their organization. That collective trust, clarity, and focus is essential for people to use the output reliably and rigorously for their decision-making.

The facilitation of the Strategic Alignment Process™ provides the necessary level of collective engagement, participation, and a high-quality decision-making process that produces distillation of the team's best thinking, quickly and powerfully. The quality of ownership that the Strategic Alignment Process™ produces is key to its success and difficult to attain with traditional strategic planning processes.

Another large part of the success of the Strategic Alignment Process™ comes from effectively designing a structure through which the decision-making builds. The process builds so organically that it deepens engagement at every step. Each step of the Strategic Alignment Process™ both clarifies a critical decision-making factor and validates and strengthens the preceding elements on which each step is based. This iterative process reinforces the trust and confidence in, clarity of, and connection to the output being generated.

Unlike many strategic planning experiences, the Strategic Alignment Process™ stands apart as a faster and more engaging experience. Generating the deep thinking to effectively define these fundamental foundations for great decision-making is one of two valuable results.

The other result of immense importance comes from the way the Strategic Alignment Process™ is conducted. The nature of the key decisions being addressed, as well as the way that these questions are structured and answered, produces a powerfully collaborative team building experience. You will read more about the facilitation that drives the process in the next chapter, a highly effective process for decision-making of any kind, at any time.

WHEN ELEMENTS ARE WEAK OR MISSING

In producing outstanding decision-making, each of the elements in the Strategic Alignment Process™ matters. They also integrate with and influence the other distinctions. Missing any one of these elements produces a weakened infrastructure, limiting the overall coherence and impact of the decision-making.

Let's consider what happens when a key element of the high-quality decision-making process is lacking.

Missing the Vision makes the ultimate picture of success a hazy blur, or a blank screen with no image at all. The lack of a compelling and engaging picture of the ultimate destination that **inspires people in the present** makes it harder to engage them in focusing on what is really possible. Your best people, want a compelling Vision. Done well, a Vision generates a deep level of engagement.

The typical, weak default for poor or missing Visionist making Goals the predominant focus point. When this occurs, it means that it is extremely likely that the chosen Goals are made up, going to be controversial, and hard to form a real consensus around – are based on someone's agenda. The Goals will also lack validation by not having a clear reason that explains why these chosen objectives are the best possible choices. This results in resistance to or a lack of true consensus in support of achieving them.

Missing the Mission makes the rationale for why choices are being made very weak. This inability to validate a decision with a truly compelling reason weakens the ability to strongly and collectively explain why your team should buy in and commit to the decision.

The typical, weak default for poor or missing Mission is arguing about what Strategies are the best. This becomes a fight for power among the participants, who are often left leveraging their position authority to influence the choice of Strategies. This creates a fight about how to get things done, rather than thoughtfully and collectively defining the rationale for all-important choices.is then unlikely there will be sustainable, decision-making.

Missing or specious Goals makes the ability to measure progress very difficult. The "Goal lines" disappear, replaced by temporary, frequently changing, often inadequate or inappropriate benchmarks. The problem in doing things this way is that, even when achieved, weak Goals disconnect your people from a coherent and compelling sense of progress and accomplishment.

The typical, weak default for poor or missing Goals is ever chang-ing metrics that annoy and frustrate your people. This ends up deflect-ing them from consistently focusing on what really matters. That in turn has them losing passion and persistence for, and commitment to, the made-up metrics. This happens because every accomplishment ends up being replaced almost immediately with another one. Each succes-sive substitution that lacks inspiring coherence in the minds of your peo-ple progressively diminishes their commitment to the ever-changing metrics.

Missing or poor Strategies makes it nearly impossible to get the best and most appropriate action plans executed. Lacking the struc-ture for how to go about achieving the chosen objectives produces random and usually unproductive activity – which is another great way to frustrate your people.

The typical, weak default for poor or missing Strategies is blaming and finger-pointing about who and what is responsible for the failure to accomplish the Goals. When your people in different departments do not have an agreed upon set of organization-wide Strategies, managers in different divisions will typically prioritize their own, smaller group choices.

This is one of the ways silos form and get perpetuated. They tend to arise from a lack of agreement across teams or divisions as to what is really most important in service of the greater good. When these discrepancies of decision-making are not corrected, the divergence deepens, the intensity of protecting one's group – instead of the greater good – increases, and the overall organization suffers.

As you can see, each of these elements plays an important role in the creation of a meaningful structure for effective decision-mak-ing. One of the critical points to reinforce here is that the most often lacking elements among these processes are sound and well-agreed-upon reasons for why to choose a Goal or Strategy. You now know that is the very essence of your Vision and Mission The absence or weakness of your leadership team's explanation for **why** your choices make the best sense results in a lack of full commitment.

Success is much more likely when your people know why you are focusing on the Goals you are challenging them to attain and the

Strategies that you believe are the best ways to achieve these Goals. Understanding what is most important is massively enhanced by knowing why these decisions are the best choices of what to accomplish. A focus on a well-defined and explained Goal allows your people to join in the search for the best ways to attain those outcomes.

These three questions are the best structured, most effective, and ultimately most efficient framework for maximizing engagement, accomplishment, performance, and results. They are also the basis for your best decision-making:

- ✧ What is most important?
- ✧ Why are these the best choices of what is most important?
- ✧ How can we best accomplish these outcomes?

Along with delivering highly desirable results, the level of commitment and the assumption of responsibility your people will give you is highest with these elements spelled out, structured clearly, well-communicated, and supported consistently.

These elements of great decision-making and enhanced engagement also support and validate each other. This is another one of the ways the structure of the Strategic Alignment Process™ ensures it rigorously provides clarity, coherence, and comprehensive alignment for everyone.

CHAPTER 8

FACILITATING DISTILLATION OF BEST THINKING

"Great leaders are almost always great simplifiers, who can cut through argument, debate, and doubt to offer a solution everybody can understand."

General Colin Powell

What drives the effectiveness of the Strategic Alignment Process™ is both:

✧ The impeccable structure of the essential elements for superior decision-making

✧ The "Distillation of Best Thinking" facilitation process that creates collaboration, understanding, and teamwork

The "Distillation of Best Thinking" process is built on the fundamentals that ensure the best considerations and conversations are being had. What makes this an outstanding and highly trustworthy process is that its design produces the following:

✧ Everyone participates at a meaningful level at every step of the way

✧ Clear individual thinking and input is generated at every step

✧ Small group processing requires that everyone is heard. As people recognize quickly, it is much harder to dominate a small group than a large group
  ○ When you need the vote of only a few colleagues to get your idea moved forward, the level of civility and respect goes way up. Compare this to holding a large group hostage by someone droning on and on

✧ Once each of the small groups have distilled their best thinking, they share their best final output of 3 to 4 points on a flip chart with the large group
  ○ Additionally, in the small groups they have had a chance to work with their colleagues.
  ○ When the group is, they really get to know, understand, and dialogue with each other. This produces a deeper level of connection and engagement that rarely happens when all the decisions are made in a large group
  ○ This process produces a deep and excellent business-focused, team building experience

✧ As everyone reviews all of the small group feedback in the larger group, typically 25% to 50% of the reported output is overlapping or redundant which already shows how much cohesion and consistency exists
  ○ These overlapping redundancies are then removed, leaving a manageable group of best thinking options for the large group to choose the ultimate top priorities from

✧ The ensuing large group discussion ensures that:
  ○ The large group is working with the very best ideas that have already been brought forward through the small group distillation process
  ○ The large group discussions are focused on discussing a reasonable number of already well thought through ideas
  ○ Participants are working through the meaning of the key decisions being discussed. This is done by having the participants really get to know and understand what is meant by the ideas being collectively discussed and chosen. This

is truly essential for collective understanding, engagement, and ownership.

- ○ Everyone feels ownership at a higher level of commitment – as the top choices in this process typically have overwhelming consensus. This is usually in the range of 75% to 100% agreement on the top chosen decisions
- ✧ Ultimately, having processed output in an individual, small group, and large group sequence, participants feel like they have considered a wide range of issues deeply and long enough to be happy and comfortable with their decisions.

Even though they have considered a wide range of ideas, this **Distillation of Best Thinking** process is much faster than any other processing methodology. This is especially true for rapidly coming up with such important and significant decisions that will inform and drive the organization's decision-making, performance, and results.

Getting to clarity and agreement among the group rapidly, yet without short-changing the process of considering all meaningful options, is critically important. This process distills best thinking quickly and powerfully, working within these typical time frames for each stage of the decision-making:

- ✧ **Personal clarification** typically takes only 2 to 3 minutes. This is more than enough for individual participants to bullet point their answers on a sheet of paper
- ✧ **Small group clarification** typically requires only 12 to 18 minutes. When handled efficiently, this is what is needed for a small group to hear, discuss, and distill their top 3 answers from among everyone's personal points and put them on a flip chart to present to the large group
  - ○ Three to five the perfect number of participants for a small group, although more can be accommodated easily when working with very large groups
- ✧ **Large group clarification and finalization** typically takes 20 to 40 minutes per element. This allows the large group to discuss the meaning of the options and distill their choice of the best and most valuable points

What this means is that even a very significant and important deci-sion can be generated in under an hour. Larger groups(over 20, for instance)may take just a little longer because there would be more smaller groups to present their findings, and more people in the large group discussion. We have facilitated the Strategic Alignment Process™ successfully in groups as large as 300 people in one day. Remember the adage that makes this work: **Clarity of outcome and quality of process produces the most outstanding results.**

Being able to get people to distill their best thinking quickly and collaboratively really does raise the engagement level. So many people go into a meeting with low expectations, based upon dozens of poorly run and rarely productive meeting experiences. Too often, strategic planning sessions are among the least enjoyable, least pro-ductive, and most painful meetings people are forced to participate in. Breaking that mold in a dramatic and enjoyable way opens partici-pants up to greater creativity, collaboration, consensus, and collective excitement to do more than they imagined was possible.

Participants leave a Strategic Alignment Process™ session with deep clarity, strong agreement, and common focus, inspired and excited to move forward. This not the typical result of most meetings. The perspective coming out of the Strategic Alignment Process™ is that the team participants are more open to continuing to engage with each other. **There is a much stronger desire and commitment to stay aligned and on track, because people can see and feel the beginning of a major upgrade of their collective functioning.**

Like all important and lasting results, what was developed in the session needs to be supported, nourished, and sustained. The enthu-siasm and collaboration that was a hallmark of the process makes it much easier to continue building on the momentum.

WHY POOR DECISION-MAKING IS SO PREDOMINANT

Why is decision-making so slow, poorly done, and often incompre-hensible to many people in organizations?

When decision-making lacks coherence, it is extremely difficult to do much with. Your people are left wondering how to decide what they should actually do. The result is that managers and leaders end up making decisions that should be made by their people, and telling their people what to do, often without any coherence or consistency. This leads to everyone being unhappy:

- ✧ The leaders complain they have to make all the decisions, which results in their workload increasing and complaints that their people are not taking enough responsibility
- ✧ The people complain there is a lack of consistency in what they are being asked to do, which results in needing more guidance to know what direction to move in

A lack of clear decision-making makes it nearly impossible for people to have confidence in what they are doing. They then avoid responsibility because they are not clear what to be responsible for. Not only do they not know what the basis for good decision-making is, the basis seems to change all the time. The concern becomes more about how to avoid a problem or mistake.

Knowing what the most important priorities are – and why they are important – produces immense clarity and focus. Without this kind of clarity and focus, it is not surprising that there is an over-reliance on senior leaders and managers telling their people what to do. Then that produces a serious reduction in the amount of responsibility, initiative, and engagement likely to be found in that organization.

These are the organizations where what is most important can be changing week to week, and the Strategies coming down from above can change daily. These are also the organizations where leaders complain about how hard it is to make change happen. Of course, their people are complaining that change is a daily occurrence, so why change today if things will just change again tomorrow?

When there is no clarity about what really matters, and no clear ways to validate why any choices are the best ones, no one knows what to base a decision on. When there is a clarity of Vision and Mission, people are able to evaluate every choice against a significant and meaningful set of criteria. This allows anyone to explain their decisions with a sound basis for achieving a valuable outcome.

By being able to think about the most important outcomes and why they matter, the task of figuring out how to make the result happen becomes massively simplified. The basis for good decision-making is obvious and applicable. In this way anyone in an organization can know they are using a sound basis for good decision-making, since the criteria:

◇ Make sense
◇ Are clearly spelled out
◇ Are consistent across the team and organization
◇ Are validated and supported by their leadership and teammates

Clarity of Vision, Mission, and Values is key to effectively driving the basis for decision-making down the organization. Adding clear measurements of progress and success your Goals provides your people additional valuable tools for decision-making. When your people know what is most important to accomplish and have a framework for why those would be the choices of what is most important, decision-making can be effectively done at every level of your organization.

CHAPTER 9

THE POWER OF STRATEGIC ALIGNMENT

*"Management is efficiency in climbing
the ladder of success.
Leadership determines whether the ladder
is leaning against the right wall."*
Stephen Covey

The power of a coherent decision-making process transforms what would otherwise be inefficient effort into insight, inspiration, and impact!

Once you recognize the critically important levers of decision-making, building the foundational framework becomes clearer and easier. Fight off the impulse to fling ideas against the wall and see what sticks – which is always a poor substitute for clarity of outcome and quality of process. Use these principles that guide all great decision-making for the fastest and best results.

Defining and applying the underlying, internal key elements of great decision-making requires engaging your Identity, Values, Beliefs, and Rules. These provide an impeccable foundation of well-grounded components to make your most important decisions regarding Vision, Mission, Goals, and Strategies. In fact, once you have done the hard work of ensuring your underlying foundation is well-grounded, coherent, and attuned to your organization, the ease and speed with which your Vision, Mission, Goals, and Strategies can be clarified is astounding.

So many **organizations and leadership teams struggle to make decisions on these important decision drivers. That is a sure sign that they lack agreement on these most effective levers of decision-making**. The likelihood that decisions made during the Strategy wrestling match will mean much many weeks and months later is extremely low. That also means that the likelihood of success in achieving outstanding results is pretty small. You know what happens when you walk out of a meeting marked by struggle and lack of true agreement and alignment. You know that the trajectory of energy, enthusiasm, engagement, and effectiveness is already limited, and likely turning even further downwards quickly.

This is absolutely unnecessary! The determination of an organization's Identity, Values, and Beliefs via the Strategic Alignment Process™ is a highly engaging teambuilding experience. Creating a basis for decision-making through this process produces a strong:

➢ Coming together of your people
➢ Deepening understanding of each other
➢ Discovering of the highest common ground
➢ Building of collective ownership
➢ Installing of inspiring touchpoints that grow in impact over time
➢ Enhancement of team camaraderie and mutual support

Done well, this decision-making process creates a strong team building and bonding experience, all while addressing your most important business issues. Where most strategic planning events tend to create separation and can lead to silo thinking and operating, **the Strategic Alignment Process™ sequence ensures cohesion, collaboration, improved communication, and collective ownership.**

In today's fast moving, fast changing business environment, the lack of alignment at the senior level gets amplified, as you move down the organization. Enhanced agreement and alignment at the executive level builds a level of trust, dialogue, and commonality of focus that permeates the organization a key characteristic of the most successful leadership teams and organizations.

If you fail to have alignment on the Vision, Mission, and Goals, how can you collaborate around the Strategies that will drive maximum success? How will you and your people be able to work out issues as they arise if you are missing the collectively agreed upon important touchstones of decision-making?

Having built a collegially arrived at core set of decision-making principles, decisions have longer lasting and higher quality reliability and application over time. Rather than deteriorating under pressure, well derived Vision, Mission, and Goals become stronger, more resilient, and more reliable over time. They resonate in harmony with the Identity, Values, and Empowering Beliefs of the organizations further deepening the cultural connection and congruence.

These are the qualities that the best decision-making consistently provides:

- ◇ Consistent clarity about what is most important
- ◇ Strong explanations why choices about what is most important make sense
- ◇ Fast creation of Strategies for success because the objectives are clear and well understood
- ◇ Powerful ways to communicate to everyone the **what, why,** and **how**
- ◇ Easier delegation, because the criteria for success, rationale for these metrics, and ways to achieve these results are so clear, well aligned, and logical

Remember that "Clarity Is Power." Nothing is more powerful than an organization that is clear and focused on what the most important and highest impact results look like and can then explain why these really matter. The Strategic Alignment Process™ accelerates effective performance and elevates meaningful results because it:

- ◇ Takes less time than the traditional process, providing plenty of positive energy to engage in quality conversations and decision-making
- ◇ Brings people together in service of the greater good (the opposite of silo thinking and turf-protection)
- ◇ Generates overwhelming consensus on all key decisions

✧ Clarifies what really matters and is most important to focus on
✧ Explains why these choices of what really matters are the best ones
✧ Provides clear and simple ways to communicate these important decisions that provide the basis for better decision-making throughout the organization
✧ Allows everyone to see how their actions are connected to achieving important Goals that in turn are key to fulfilling the Vision and Mission

The growth of engagement, the elevation of enthusiasm, the embracing of responsibility, and the acceleration of well thought through actions in the service of enhanced results are every leader wants. When you provide your people with clear, comprehensible, and aligned Vision, Mission, Goals, and Strategies, the likelihood of this happening is exponentially elevated.

This is what every great leader, executive team, and organization needs and thrives on. Are you ready to make it happen in your organization?

WORKING THE STRATEGIC ALIGNMENT PROCESS™

*"Excellence is never an accident. It is always the result of
High intention, sincere effort and intelligent execution.
It represents the wise choice of many alternatives –
choice, not chance, determines your destiny."*

Aristotle

CHAPTER 10

EXECUTING THE STRATEGIC ALIGNMENT PROCESS™

*"I am not a product of my circumstances.
I am a product of my decisions."*
Stephen Covey

An important part of successfully designing any meeting requires getting your people engaged and enthusiastic about what is going to happen.

Not many people relish the thought of a day (or often two or three days) working on Vision, Mission, Goals, and Strategies. Of course this is primarily due to the terrible experiences and poor results they have experienced in past planning sessions. They recoil at the memories of: the political horse-trading among the team; the push and pull of people wanting departmental–specific favors that would disadvantage other groups; the vague and vacuous fights over wordsmithing; and the dissipation of most good intentions in a matter of days after the session.

That means you and your team have put out a lot of effort for an exceedingly low amount of meaningful results. Sometimes it is so bad it even takes quite a bit of time to recover and come back together as a team that can work together well.

Most strategic planning sessions last 2 or 3 or even 4 days, even when they do not or cannot come to a meaningful consensus on the key levers of decision-making. In fact, most strategic planning sessions end up missing a meaningful Vision and Mission, which are critically important distinctions. Many times, the articulation of what they accomplish is weak, and even more often does not produce a cohesive alignment. Then comes the battering-by-wordsmithing attempts to make what they have at least a little palatable.

There is a better way.

PREPARING FOR THE SESSION

First of all, it makes sense to prime your people prior to the meeting. This is valuable both to get them to look forward to a much better experience than they have been used to and to gather insights that will support the success of the session. Consistent with our whole approach to communicating as a leader, that is best done by a compelling message outlining the most valuable expected outcomes of the session – and why they matter.

This is where it is important to start differentiating between a Strategic Alignment Process™ session and the typical decision-making meeting. Doing that is important, since so many people have had terrible experiences working on Vision and Mission, as well as doing strategic planning. Start by focusing on what is most important to accomplish and why these are such valuable and meaningful choices, including confirming that:

- ✧ We will collectively come to an agreement on what is most important for the organization
- ✧ Everyone's input will be heard due to the way the meeting will be run
- ✧ We will be building highest common denominator agreement and consensus among the whole group – and wheeling and dealing to arrive at a lowest common denominator decision
- ✧ We will be communicating the decisions to the whole organization in comprehensible and compelling way

✧ We will be focused on providing the decision-making team and the organization with a clarity of focus that will lead to a highly successful impact on performance and results

✧ We are going to clarify the most important basis for decision-making in the organization going forward that everyone can understand and work with

These are the results that matter and will be appreciated by your people. These are the results that an overwhelming consensus of agreement will produce. These are the results that will be worth leadership's time, energy, and engagement. In fact, this may well be the most valuable day of the year in ensuring your organization's clarity, focus on what really matters, and making the decisions that will most impact your short- and long-term results.

We suggest that the number of people you involve in the session be as large and representative of the key contributors across your organization as possible. The Strategic Alignment Process™ can be run effectively with as few as 3 and as many as 300 people. Most often a good group size that provides for significant input from across all the important parts of a company is 12 to 24 people. Again, the number of people attending in no way inhibits the quality of conversation. This is another reason why quality of design really does matter.

A preliminary survey will be advantageous done prior to the session. This is part of priming the pump, both because it provides excellent insight for the facilitators and your team, and it piques interest by the participants to see what the commonalities are. The survey questions are intended to see how much clarity and cohesion, as well as differences of opinion, already exists by asking:

1. What are the most important results you want from the meeting?
2. What are the most important results the organization should be focused on achieving in the next 12 months (or 24 months, whichever is most appropriate)?
3. What are the strengths, capabilities, talents, and resources that support achieving these results?

4. What are the limitations, obstacles, challenges, and liabilities that could keep us from achieving these results?
5. What else do we need to know to support you and the organization in being as successful as possible?

The responses are compiled and distilled to identify the most common answers and themes. These are shared early in the Strategic Alignment Process™ session.

STRATEGIC ALIGNMENT PROCESS™ SESSION STEPS

The sequence of the session matters. By building upon the elements in a certain order, a foundation of clarity and confidence in the group's decisions gets stronger and stronger. Additionally, after the element of Identity is worked through, each successive section becomes easier and easier. Once the Purpose, Vision, and Mission are in place, determining the Goals and Strategies becomes enormously simplified and a wider range of options than most teams usually have to work with.

STEP 1 – VALUES:

While the first element in the Identity, Values, Beliefs, and Rules sequence and the most important internal element to build upon is Identity, we always start with the Values. The reason for this is quite simple. Values are enormously powerful, extremely important in decision-making, and very simple to distinguish. Defining Values is a dramatic and enormously engaging experience that can move smoothly and quickly. This process also generates meaningful momentum and confidence among the group in their ability to do significant work together. That successful work prepares them for continuing to work on each of the successive elements.

The fundamental question regarding Values is:

✧ "What is most important for us to commit to being, honoring, and holding as essential in order for us to be as effective and successful as possible"

The conversation about Values also has two distinct levels. These are differentiated as to what I call Means Values versus Ends Values. Simply put, Means Values are **things or actions** that people hold as important in order to achieve some important feeling or state of being. For example, sales growth, better customer satisfaction, and getting more media attention are common Means Values.

When things or actions are offered as what people value, you need to ask a follow up question: "What is most important about (use one of their Means Values) for instance "improved sales"

Ends Values answers could be a feeling of respect, recognition, security, success, passion, excellence, creativity, connection, impact, and so forth. All of these could be states of being, feelings that the team wants to experience. Most important about experiencing these Ends Values is that they motivate the participants to strive for even greater success and effectiveness.

Here are some real sets of Values of different organizations with whom I have worked:

✧ Integrity, Focus, Collaborative, Adaptable, Driven

✧ Excellence, Clarity, Recognition, Contribution, Effective

✧ Excellence, Integrity, Adaptable, Innovative, Respected

While these might share an Ends Value in common, can you see what a different kind of culture each of these organizations would have just based upon their Values? Even though the first and third groups are both very strong science-based organizations and share two Values in common, you can see that they are very different in what they value and want to be. The second group is a significant non-profit foundation. Even though their top Value is the same as the third group, they are quite different, as expressed by the other Values.

The process of clarifying an organization's Values provides a structure for defining what really matters and drives that company. This already is tuning the focus and attention of the company in profoundly important ways. And this is just the first step.

STEP 2 – IDENTITY

Identity is the most powerful force for congruence in people, groups, teams, organizations, and even nations. That is, the Identity you claim as an individual, group, team, or organization – is what you will seek to maintain with the greatest congruence and consistency.

Throughout history people have identified themselves and where they belong by:

⋄ Gender
⋄ Religion
⋄ Nationality
⋄ Profession
⋄ Education
⋄ Neighborhood
⋄ Work organizations
⋄ Relationship status
⋄ Social group or club
⋄ Favorite sports team
⋄ Political party or leaning
⋄ Generation

I'm sure you could identify many more forms of affinity and connection.

All of these create a sense of belonging at a deep level. The depth of belonging depends upon how much someone associates with a particular Identity. **The stronger the affiliation and connection to the Identity, the stronger the need to act in accordance with what it means to be "that kind of person."**

On the negative side, so many wars have been fought over differences in nationality and religion. These are two of the most ancient and strongest Identities that tend to reject the differences of others.

In a more current and corporate sense, **how much connection people feel to what their organization claims as their key descriptors affects how strongly they act in ways that are consistent with what it means to be a member of that organizational Identity.**

For example, organizations known for their strong sense of Identity as we have seen, a key driver of a strong culture– are Google, FedEx, Apple, Microsoft, Merck, American Express, the Red Cross, and many other smaller, strongly self-identified groups.

What is also remarkable to observe is how organizations tend to deteriorate when they stop acting in ways that are consistent with their sense of Identity. Hewlett Packard is an excellent case in point. Starting in that legendary garage in Palo Alto, California, HP grew to be one of the most iconic organizations in the world. In 2009 they were the largest tech company in the world, #9 on the Fortune 500 list that year, and much bigger than Microsoft and Apple. However, they lost their way and the clarity of their iconic Identity as they were buying other companies, confusing themselves and the market as to who they were and what they stood for.

Magellan Fund investing guru Peter Lynch coined the term "diworsification" to describe this kind of poor and inefficient diversification. Over time they separated into divisions, sold parts of themselves off, ended up with leaders who were fired for improprieties, and turned out being quite different from being identified as an iconic and legendary company.

While still around over 80 years later, the legendary Identity that was HP is not what it once was. The Identity it owns now is far less dynamic and iconic. It is not the legend it once was. Here is how HP ranked in the Fortune 500, along with their revenues every 10 years between 1989 and 2019 *(the revenues reported in their Fortune 500 listing may be different from the actual fiscal year calculations because of how Fortune does their calculations):*

- ✧ 1989: #39 with $9.8B in revenues
- ✧ 1999: #14 with $44.6B in revenues
- ✧ 2009: #9 with $118.4B (HP was the largest tech company; Microsoft was #35 at $60.4B; Apple was #71 at $32.5B)
- ✧ 2019: #55 with $58.5 B. (Apple was #3 at $294.1B; Microsoft was #26 at $110.4B)

THE POWER OF IDENTITY

The strength, drive, and impact that an organization's Identity can produce is often not tapped into or used as it could be. In fact, most companies fail to really consider who they are beyond their marketing slogans. However, marketing slogans are rarely meaningful Identities and hardly affect the culture of an organization. One of the most important aspects of an effective Identity is that it pervades the culture.

Who you are as a team or organization ought to produce a strong coherence and connection for your people. This strong Identity coherence affects how your people think about and hold themselves with clients and in the broader world. Obviously, the opposite is also true – a weak or inadequate Identity leaves everyone to make up their own idea about what their organization stands for. This is a common cause of lack of alignment, agreement, and consistent action.

The problem in defining Identity is you cannot just ask: "Who are you?" Most people would not know what to respond and almost certainly have given little thought to having a well-considered answer. The power of Identity resides in a deeper, more empathic, and neurological level of awareness. However, any statement of Identity is often colored with vague, sometimes competing, and often uninspiring random thoughts. That is totally unnecessary simply because most organizations never address this consciously and coherently.

It is important to have a clear and compelling Identity to manifest the quality of leadership that comes from a strong strategic alignment. This absolutely requires a clarity about who a team or organization is.

THE PROCESS OF GENERATING IDENTITY

Identity, done well, builds a deep-seated and powerful foundation of coherence for any organization and its people. This is one of the most commonly missing core elements of decision-making. The good news is that the Strategic Alignment Process™ makes it to access because of the approach taken.

Your Identity could feel like a brand, but it is significantly more powerful than that. It comes from how people, clients, colleagues, the market, the media, your families, and everyone who counts what I call an "important constituency" sees you. Given that Identity is usually buried deep in the unarticulated subconscious, it is critical to move to making some conscious choices here.

The best and fastest way to bring forth the strongest and most compelling Identity is to do two very specific things:

✧ First, adopt the perspectives of the key constituencies that matter noted above. We do this because it is easier to get a sense of who we are by referencing what we think others think about us

   ○ Of course, we are talking only about the good, uplifting, positive and meaningful thoughts they have about us

✧ Second, use the neurological power of memory to produce a stronger sense of reality.

   ○ Our memory of the past is of course much more real to us than what has yet to be created in the future

   ○ By looking back **from the future,** what you see will feel much more real than looking out into the future to imagine what might happen in the coming years

This is how we use what I call the "neurological hack." First by imagining that we are walking out to 3 years in the future and turning around and looking back over that time, our subconscious accepts that this could have really happened. This trick of neuroscience allows for a more open, creative, and richer perspective than simply starting from the present and looking forward.

By imagining what all the constituencies that matter to you might say about who you have been for them, you can better understand:

✧ How they might see you

✧ What you might have done for them

✧ What you might mean to them

his actually allows you to conceptualize what could be their point of view. This frees you from having to feel like you had to have done something that really happened. It becomes more of a possibility that you could have really been or done almost anything in the future.

This produces a very compelling sense of who you are from the point of view of others. However, the truth of the process is that the only point of view we actually possess is ours. Even though we are putting ourselves in the shoes of our key constituencies, it is our perspectives and possibilities that are being captured. This "neurological " enables you to engage deeply, and effectively forth a strong collection of Identities to choose from.

One of the statements that produces both a laugh and a recognition I often share at this point is that "Multiple Identities are good. Multiple personalities are not." As individuals, we all hold many Identities: spouse, parent, son or daughter, friend, professional, expert, leader, manager, star performer, athlete, and so on. A strong organization usually has at least a few powerful Identities– often 3 that resonate powerfully.

This practice of consciously choosing the most compelling Identities is one of the processes that regularly produces an organization's strongest revelations. It opens up much larger possibilities and perspectives and does it from a very powerful position. These are key distinctions that affect culture, recruiting, marketing, sales, and client relationships.

Upon completing this section, you now have established 2 of the 3 most powerful forces of human and organizational decision-making – Identity and Values. It is time to address that third most important element– Purpose.

THE PROCESS OF CHOOSING PURPOSE

While the power of Purpose is routinely talked about and considered one of the most powerful forces for great decision-making (it is!), most people come to it in very roundabout ways. Most of the literature about creating Purpose considers all sorts of tangential guided explorations like: What do you love? What have you found rewarding?

What do people say about you? What do you aspire to? Why do you care about the things you do?

I am sorry to say this is a random and often unfulfilling exploration, especially when the clearest, most direct foundations of Purpose are very straightforward and available.

Purpose shows up in the most grounded yet inspiring way when you operate at the intersection of Identity and Values. If you are working on the ultimate **why** an organization exists (its Purpose), what more compelling foundation would deliver that insight than the intersection of who you are (Identity), and what you hold as most important (Values)?

I define Purpose as the 360-degree, comprehensive reason(s) why you exist. The "why you " could be for an individual, a team, an organization, an industry, or any other entity. When we ask what an organization's ultimate Purpose is, we are seeking to provide the deepest and most profound reasons why anyone would want to be involved with or support this entity.

This overriding **why** also provides very important guidance. The Purpose validates why all of the choices, decisions, and actions that end up being made make sense. That means that choices, decisions, and actions must align with and support **why** this entity would do anything.

The stated Purpose of many organizations is weak, missing, or misunderstood. Finding an individual's or an organization's Purpose has too often become an exercise in throwing something against the wall and seeing what sticks. Are the results of this kind of process compelling enough for you to dedicate yourself to, or ask your people to dedicate themselves to, with real conviction?

The primary reason that Purpose might be weak is that the most powerful building block – Identity – is weak or missing. That's right, without a sound and strong Identity, your Purpose would be weak, built on weak links, and missing the strongest element that guides human beings who we are. It seems like common sense to say that it is extremely difficult to know why you are here if you are not clear about who you actually are.

As you have read, the power of Vision comes from containing and integrating the 3 most powerful forces of human decision-making. How could a powerful Vision arise from a weak Identity or Purpose? Vision only has as much power as the weakest part of the it is built on.

The strength and power of Purpose is directly drawn from the strength and power of Identity and Values. The work of bringing forth these 2 essential building blocks makes the clarification of Purpose a fast and highly energizing process. It is just like building a house. Ensuring the foundation is strong and done well makes it much easier to erect the rest of the structure. Done well, you can trust your structure will stand the test of time.

The question for determining Purpose must build on Identity and Values. Here is the question that opens up your access to Purpose:

✧ "Given who we are (best to use your actual Identity statements), and what we value most (again, best to use your actual Values) why are we here"

The true depth and impact of Identity, Values, and Purpose is not just an intellectual consideration. In fact, the intellectual deliberations are the weakest considerations of all! The question above is easily answered when you tap into a deep connection of your Identity and Values. The stronger your connection to your Identity and Values, the faster and more clearly your Purpose shows up!

Many organizations have weak, marketing-driven, even inauthentic Purpose statements. However, getting to a deep and meaningful Purpose in the Strategic Alignment Process™ is a smooth and often quite dazzling experience. Most of the time the Purpose section of the session only takes 45 to 90 minutes (the longer time as a consequence of working with a larger number of people).

Clarity of Purpose, built on a powerful platform of Identity and Values, opens the door to creating a Vision of the future that provides a compelling, high impact container for focus, inspiration, alignment, and results!

CHAPTER 11

THE POWER OF VISION – WHEN DONE WELL

"Where there is no vision, the people perish."
Proverbs 29:18

"The best way to predict the future is to create it."
Abraham Lincoln

Everyone is familiar with the power of Vision as promoted by globally known leadership. It is entirely consistent with exceptional leadership to have a Vision that is compelling, memorable, and even iconic. Some well-known examples include:

⬦ Martin Luther King's vision of racism ending in the United States
⬦ Nelson Mandela's vision of abolishing apartheid (even while in prison for these views)
⬦ Mother Teresa's vision of a global movement so every person can die with dignity
⬦ John F. Kennedy's vision of the US sending a man to the moon within 10 years
⬦ Google's founders' vision of all the world's knowledge catalogued and accessible to anyone

There are many more great examples, but they all contain one commonality that makes them profoundly powerful. **Visions that work** well are built on a picture of the future that is based upon the three most powerful forces of decision-making in all of humankind: Identity, Purpose, and Values.

These three forces represent the most potent and highest impact questions that philosophers, sages, guides, and deep thinkers have asked throughout recorded history. These are the 3 most fundamental and important questions for every human being and organization – especially to guide all of their other decisions:

1. Who am I?
2. Why am I here?
3. What really matters?

These are the questions that illuminate Identity, Purpose, and Values when thoughtfully and processed. It is no wonder that when these exceptional forces for meaning and deep engagement are clearly articulated, people flock to be in alignment with them.

Only a well-honed, compelling Vision of the future can contain the power of all 3 of these elements in a single picture. By representing all 3, a Vision essentially magnifies the impact of these s by integrating them into a single, all-encompassing whole.

As powerful and compelling as a well-formed Vision is, very few companies achieve that level of impact and engagement. Most fail to have a Vision that really represents what the full manifestation of their Identity, Purpose, and Values in the future would look like. The main reason that so few companies land on a Vision of immense impact is very simple. One or more of the core elements of Identity, Purpose, and Values are missing or weak.

In working to establish a Vision of compelling meaning and impact, it is essential that each of the three core components are well-defined, congruent with the organization and its leaders, and resonate strongly. You cannot build a building worth building when the foundation is weak. You cannot build a Vision when the foundations of Identity, Purpose, and Values are weak or missing.

Even when the core elements of Identity, Purpose, and Values are well developed, inspiring, and engaging, they don't just add up to a Vision. Another reason for lacking a compelling Vision is because what is being called a Vision is in reality only a Goal or

Strategy. Calling something a Vision does not make it so. The power of Vision only exists when that picture of the future truly embodies what the Identity, Purpose, and Values, fully manifested over a period of time, would look like.

Similar to the elements of Identity, Purpose, and Values, the creation of Vision is not simply an intellectual or analytical process. It requires:

- ◇ Connection to the intention, insight, and inspiration generated by Identity, Purpose, and Values
- ◇ Integration of each of these key elements into a fully expressed, greater whole
- ◇ Willingness and openness to allow imagination and creativity to give form to what the future could look like and be

What often amazes me is that so few leaders and organizations work to bring the power of Vision to bear for their people. The profound impact of a well-formed Vision is that it encompasses and contains

While working with a significant and rapidly growing company that was a leader in their field, I had the opportunity to have a conversation with the CEO. My question to him was: "What is your vision for this company" With no hesitation and great enthusiasm he replied: "We will be a 3-billion-dollar company in 3 years."

Since I know the difference between Vision, Mission, Goals, and Strategies and was sure that no one had ever questioned his answer, I replied: "And I am sure your people come to work really excited every day."

He caught my somewhat sarcastic tone and a bit in shock he asked: "What do you mean?"

I told him that this was not a Vision. If it were a Vision it would be powerfully engaging, energizing, and get his people enthusiastic about why they were coming to work. At best it was a Goal, or perhaps only a Strategy to achieve some other goal. What the CEO's message was really telling his everyone is that his people are going to have to work hard for his glory, without knowing why. Why would they be excited about that? If his people are not inspired and engaged, how could it be a meaningful Vision?

When you are working on creating a Vision, you can pick any timeframe within which to consider what the manifestation of Identity, Purpose, and Values could look like.

The most often used time frames are 1, 3, or 5 years, but I usually suggest 3 years as a great timeframe. It is far enough away to allow for virtually anything being possible, yet close enough to allow for reasonable conjecture.

the power of Identity, Purpose, and Values. That makes the communication, integration, and alignment of an organization so much simpler and more effective. It also has real and potent impact when communicating to your clients and the marketplace. A strong and compelling Vision can be a major differentiator for a company, a market niche, or even teams within an organization.

As Albert Einstein said: "Everything should be as simple as possible, and no simpler." A well-defined Vision holds the impact of those questions human beings have asked since the beginning of time. What could be more compelling?

Below are some excellent examples of Visions from well-known companies. Notice how each one affects you. Can you see how their Vision has given rise to their whole business model? Do you see how **the articulation they created of what they see in the future speaks to who they are even more than what they do?**

That is also one of the most significant ways Visions and Missions differ. The Vision shows you a picture of the future, while the Missions tell you the big reasons why you choose to do what you do.

There is a difference between a Vision and Mission, even though they both provide important insights into why something matters. However, they do it in different and significant ways.

- ◇ Vision answers the question of "What will we see in the future that explains:
  - ○ Why it is so important to be who we are,
  - ○ Know why we are here, and
  - ○ What we must hold as most important to make that future happen?
- ◇ Mission answers the question of "Why do we do what we do:
  - ○ Consistent with what we hold as most important, and
  - ○ What we believe is possible when we are at our best?"

Both are important answers to the key question about why our choices of what to focus on being and doing are our best choices. However the nuance of difference is quite meaningful. Both are valuable, and each serves to engage people deeply. The picture that a Vision paints can give a seemingly impossible or improbable future a compelling sense of possibility, or even reality.

The deep and meaningful power of Mission shows up in knowing "why we make the decisions we do." This Why is the most powerful provider of inspiration and motivation to make something happen. Having a consistent and compelling reason Why you are doing something provides a unique kind of drive. Done well it even works to keep us committed to persevering and thriving in difficult and challenging times.

If you were to do a search you would end up finding that most of what companies and organizations call their Visions and Missions are actually neither. They do not provide a compelling picture of the future, nor a compelling reason why they do what they do. Now that you know about the power of the elements that drive Visions and Missions you can see the deficiencies in their typical statements.

EXAMPLES OF VISIONS AND MISSIONS

Below are some of the better Vision and Mission statements. These are strong foundations that provide a basis for clarity and compelling engagement which is why they matter! You can also see the differences in well-structured Visions and Missions.

VISIONS:

> CATERPILLAR: *"A world in which all people's basic need – such as shelter, clean water, sanitation, food, and reliable power – are fulfilled in an environmentally sound way, by a company that improves the quality of the environment and the communities where we live and work."*

> FEEDING AMERICA: *"A hunger free America."*

> FERRARI: *"Italian excellence that makes the world dream."*

➢ GOOGLE: *"Provide access to the world's information in one click."*

➢ HABITAT for HUMANITY: *"A world where everyone has a decent place to live."*

➢ IKEA: *"Affordable solutions for better living."*

➢ OXFAM: *"A just world without poverty."*

➢ SAVE the CHILDREN: *"A world in which every child attains the right to survival, protection, development, and participation."*

➢ TEACH for AMERICA: *"One day, all children in this nation will have the opportunity to attain an excellent education."*

➢ ZOOM: *"Video communications empowering people to accomplish more."*

MISSIONS:

➢ AARP: *"To enhance quality of life for all as we age."*

➢ AMAZON: *"To be earth's most customer centric company, where people can find and discover anything they might want to buy online."*

➢ AVON: *"To be the company that best understands and satisfies the product, service, and self-fulfillment needs of women – globally."*

➢ CISCO: *"Changing the way we work, live, play and learn."*

➢ DATADOG: *"To bring sanity to IT Management."*

➢ DISNEY: *"To delight our customers, employees, and shareholders by relentlessly delivering the platform and technology advancements that become essential to the way we work and live."*

➢ FEEDING AMERICA: *"To feed America's hungry through a nationwide network of member food banks and engage our country in the fight to end hunger."*

➢ GOOGLE: *"To organize the world's information and make it universally accessible and useful."*

➢ JETBLUE: *"To inspire humanity—both in the air and on the ground."*

➢ MICROSOFT: *"To help people around the world realize their full potential."*

➢ NATURE CONSERVANCY: *"Saving the last great places."*

➢ NIKE: *"To bring inspiration and innovation to every athlete in the world."* (For Nike, *"If you have a body you are an athlete."*)

➢ PHILIPS: *"Improving people's lives through meaningful innovation."*

➢ SAMSUNG: *"Inspire the world. Create the future."*

➢ SOUTHWEST AIRLINES: *"To provide the highest quality of customer service delivered with a sense of warmth, friendliness, individual pride and company spirit."*

➢ TED: *"To spread ideas."*

➢ TESLA: *"To accelerate the world's transition to sustainable energy."*

Very often leaders and organizations fail to differentiate a Vision from a Mission. Most often they mislabel them, even calling a Strategy or Goal their Vision or Mission. When each of these key decisions are built on their appropriate foundations, the power of each grows, integrates seamlessly, enhances each other, and produces a well-aligned, highly coherent basis for excellent decision-making.

Most important, they provide a foundational precision that supports excellence in the decision-making process. This is essential to ensure the coherence and alignment of organizational Goals and Strategies.

CHAPTER 12

PROCESSING BELIEFS, MISSIONS, GOALS, AND STRATEGIES

*"Perfection of means and confusion of ends
seem to characterize our age."*
Albert Einstein

CHOOSING EMPOWERING BELIEFS

The power of Beliefs is quite strong. Beliefs energize adherence to religions, political parties, social groups, and organizational structures. They are instrumental building blocks in determining what people look at and see. They act as lens through which people see. There is an old axiom that people tend to see what they are looking for.

To prove this truth for yourself, try this experiment. Work with any group you like (professional colleagues, sports team, family members, social friends), and follow these steps:

◇ Start by telling people to stand and wait for your instructions
◇ Now tell them they have 5 seconds to find as many things as they can around them that are *(slow to a short stop of 3 seconds)* Green!
◇ Count down 5 seconds, and then ask everyone to close their eyes
◇ Once everyone has closed their eyes, <u>slowly</u> say the following (with the pause at the right point):

- ✧ "Raise your hands if you found at least 4 things that were *(slow to a short stop of 4 seconds* – Blue!"
- ✧ After everyone moans and complains, ask them to open their eyes, look around, and find as many things as they can that are Blue in the next 5 seconds
- ✧ Count down 5 seconds and ask everyone to close their eyes
- ✧ Once everyone has closed their eyes, <u>slowly</u> say the following (with the pause at the right point): "Raise your hands if you found at least 4 things that were *(slow to a short stop of 4 seconds)* – Red!"

Now it is time to understand the impact of this exercise. First ask your group what they think the learning from this lesson is? The ultimate lesson that is powerful to understand is that we tend to find what we are looking for. And we miss everything else!

Since we find what we are looking for, it is best to be aware, thoughtful, and attuned to what is most valuable and meaningful. In the context of positive, empowering Beliefs, the question we want to answer is: "What do we believe is possible when we are being, thinking, and acting at our very best?"

This is articulated as: "What we believe is possible Having 3 to 4 powerful, positive Beliefs about what is possible when your team or organization is operating at its best provides a great basis for the next 2 steps in the process – the Mission and Goals.

CHOOSING THE MISSION

To recap: Purpose articulates the overall, all-encompassing reason that you exist and focuses on being what you aspire to be. Vision is the picture of the future when you have fully manifested your Identity, Purpose, and Values. Mission is the element most closely aligned with Purpose, yet represents the clarification of a slightly different aspect (as we started noting in the prior section).

Your Mission clarifies the foundations and reasons why you and your organization make the choices and take the actions that you do.

It is the reason why you are going to make decisions and act in certain ways fully congruent and in alignment with your Purpose and Vision. Compared to your Purpose, **your Mission tends to be more tangible, more practical, and more grounded in the way it defines why you are pursuing and acting on what you are focused on.**

There is something that I very often find in the process of conducting the Strategic Alignment Process™. When we are working on the Purpose statements, many of the possibilities raised, but not chosen at that point, are put to the side. That is because they are actually Missions and not Purpose statements. Actually defining the Mission in the process of determining the Purpose happens more than 75% of the time. This demonstrates and validates how closely aligned these are, even while they are different in their intention and utilization.

The process of choosing Mission is built upon the foundations of Values and Beliefs, in alignment with the Purpose and Vision. That means that choosing Mission requires a deep connection with the inner elements of Values and Beliefs in alignment with the Purpose and the Vision.

The question for consideration goes as follows (fill in the actual content you have already defined to this point for each element listed here):

- ✧ "Given what is most important to us (your Values), and what we believe is possible for us when operating at our best (your empowering Beliefs), and aligned fully with our Vision and Purpose – what is our primary reason why we choose to be who we are, and do what we do, that guides us as our most empowering foundation for decision-making and action?"
- ✧ Missions are articulated as: "Our Mission is to…"

CHOOSING GOALS

Driven by your Beliefs about what is possible, your Goals are the markers of what you want to focus on and achieve. Goals transition you from the **why** explanations that are built on Identity, Values,

Purpose, Vision, and Mission to a different level. Goals are the way that priorities are tracked, benchmarks are built, and measurements of accomplishment are defined. Goals identify the "What Really " that you want to focus on getting done in order to fulfill your Vision and Mission.

In fact, that is how I define Goals as the measurements of accomplishment of your Mission and Vision. If you are accomplishing your Goals, your Mission and Vision should be on the way to fulfillment as well. This is one of the most dramatic signs that your Goals make sense and the desired Strategic Alignment is in place.

One difference in dealing with Goals is how you process them. Commensurate with answering the question about what to measure success by, you are progressing to the level of thinking. This is different than the more visceral, intuitive, level of "being" decision-making discussed in the prior section Therefore, a different way to process Goals is in order.

In the context of determining what are the best measurements of accomplishments, I run a true brain-storming process to come up with our initial list for consideration. Starting with connection to your Beliefs and in alignment with your Vision and Mission (of course use the actual content you have already developed), ask:

✧ "Given what we Value and believe is possible, in alignment with our Mission and Vision – what are the best measurements of accomplishment that demonstrates we are fulfilling our Mission and Vision"

✧ The articulation for Goals is stated as: "Our most important Goals are..."

With a clear Vision and Mission, this takes 5 to 7 minutes with large groups. If there are 20 or less people, we might run a single group. With more people than that, we might split into smaller groups to conduct separate brainstorming groups. There is no discussion in the brainstorming, just collecting all the ideas being thrown out on to a flip chart or white board. Once we have exhausted the idea generation (it usually takes less than 7 minutes then we move to the next step. We distill the best choices from among the entire list.

As is typical of brainstorming sessions, half of the ideas you will generate will be useless. However, the power of brainstorming is that getting everything out often opens up access to some really good ideas. **Consistently I find that the majority of the best ideas usually come in the last one-third of the session.**

Even though about half of the ideas can be tossed out immediately, continue evaluating which are the best measurements of accomplishment of the Vision and Mission. Continue distilling your list until you have 3 potential Goals. These are the best and most important 3 from among all the others.

The last step in the Goals process is to ensure that there are meaningful measurements that are clear enough to use to monitor progress and success. Many times the top Goals make sense but may need some additional research, input, or study outside the Strategic Alignment Process™ session. Rarely does this take more than a week. However, the general framework of the top Goals should be as clear as is realistically possible and agreed to as you move on to the next section.

Once the Goals are clear, you naturally want to define how you are going to achieve them. It is time to decide the Strategies that will deliver success in achieving your Goals.

CHOOSING STRATEGIES

Strategies, those actions that are taken to achieve your Goals, are the essence of how what is most important gets accomplished. This is the point of transition from having clarified what really matters, and explained why those were the best choices of what to focus on. This is the phase where you focus on how to accomplish these important results.

What is most remarkable in observing typical strategic planning conversations is how much time and energy is spent on Strategies. If you ask most leaders what conversations take the most amount of time and generate the greatest amount of conflict, it is not Vision, Mission, or Goals, but rather Strategies.

The amazing point here is that if the Vision, Mission, and Goals are clear, agreed upon, and in alignment, the conversation about Strategies is the SHORTEST one in the Strategic Alignment Process™!

Some of the most significant reasons why Strategies are so challenging in the typical way strategic planning is done is that there is a:

⬦ Missing Vision, and/or Mission, and/or Goals
⬦ Lack of clarity about the Vision, Mission, and/or Goals
⬦ Poor alignment between the Vision, Mission, and Goals
⬦ Moving to Strategy discussions without agreement on the Vision, Mission, and/or Goals
⬦ Made up and / or a poor set of Goals, which cannot be validated or justified

If your strategic planning session feels like a free-for-all or a "death march" where people finally capitulate and agree on something just to get out of the meeting, you are planning the old-fashioned, highly ineffective, and inadequate way.

It makes sense that you start your decision-making from the foundations that are most stable, meaningful, inspiring, and reliable. But let's look at how often the key elements we base our decision-making on changes:

⬦ Tactics change as quickly as the last email, phone call, or new idea
⬦ Strategies change as often as daily, weekly, monthly – but frequently
⬦ Goals change annually or even or monthly
⬦ Mission may change every 3 to 5 years – potentially even longer may evolve –even r

When you have an important and necessary decision to make, which element would you use to validate you are making a good choice? Would you use elements that are consistently changing, or ones that are stable and lasting?

Another of the most pernicious destroyers of good decision-making is that the choices being made do not have a basis for validation. Too many otherwise smart people hop right on the hamster wheel of activity and try to outrun an issue. If it is an important issue, that rarely works. Often, ignoring or dealing poorly with an issue only serves to make its pain and consequences worse the next time it pops up.

Too many people:

◇ Substitute activity for results
◇ Substitute being busy for being smart about what is worth doing
◇ Substitute forming committees or setting up meetings for having a real process for good decision-making

It is too bad that none of these works very well.

If your Vision informs your Mission, and your Goals are excellent measurements of accomplishment of your Mission and Vision, asking the question: "How can we best achieve this Goal" should create an avalanche of ideas and options, which is exactly how we process Strategies in the Strategic Alignment Process™.

We are going to apply the same brainstorming process as we did with Goals. Choosing one Goal to work on at a time, we will do the following with each round:

◇ Brainstorm all of the possible responses to the question: "How can we best achieve this Goal?" in approximately 5 minutes
  ○ If people are still providing useful responses after 5 minutes, continue for as long as there is a flow of quality comments
◇ Review all of the options and choose the most effective and compelling ones. You want to come up with the 3 to 4 most useful, valuable, and highest impact Strategies
◇ Flesh out the selected Strategies to ensure they are clear to everyone

Doing this for each of the top 3 Goals you had chosen should take approximately 15 to 30 minutes per Goal.

When the Vision, Mission, and Goals make sense, are aligned, and agreed to, determining how to accomplish the Goals is one of the simplest activities for most groups. **However, most groups are used to jumping into action instead of thinking through what is worth acting upon.** Doing the decision-making about what is most important and useful up front makes the actions, and what can be accomplished, significantly more meaningful!

CHAPTER 13

CONTINUING THE MOMENTUM

"Earn your leadership every day."
Michael Jordan

After a thoroughly engaging Strategic Alignment Process™ session spent clarifying and integrating the critical levers of effective decision-making, lots of positive emotion. There are also serious expectations being generated. These positive sand high expectations come from:

◇ Accomplishing higher quality results in a day than similar sessions did in 2 or 3 days
◇ Collaborating and team building that takes place
◇ Engaging deeply meaningful conversations with colleagues
◇ Gaining clarity, focus, and agreement on the priorities that really matter
◇ Learning new processes for conducting better meetings
◇ Making higher quality decisions more quickly and easily
◇ Improving their executive decision-making process
◇ Believing what was done will continue to elevate and accelerate the performance and results of the team and the organization
◇ Being able to communicate the results to the rest of the organization clearly and easily

THE IMPORTANCE OF CLARITY OF OUTCOME

What is the difference between what happens after a typical strategic planning session, and the Strategic Alignment Process™?

What often happens after a traditional strategy session is that the final agreements almost immediately are being questioned, revised or even ignored. This goes on without and ensuring everyone is aware that it is happening. This occurs because the **outcomes are not truly agreed upon in a meaningful and trustworthy way**. That often happens because the process is focused on driving to a decision. By driving for a conclusion rather than focusing on producing the best, collectively owned decision the likelihood of real agreement and support is severely diminished.

Many clients complain that they have gone through so many strategic planning sessions that have failed to produce meaningful change. Once again this proves that poor process cannot produce outstanding results.

Results must align the organization's Strategies to achieve its Goals, which in turn must align with and fulfill its Mission and Vision. Nothing less than that really produces what is ultimately needed:

 ✧ Coherence in decision-making
 ✧ Comprehensive clarity about what outcomes are most important
 ✧ Clarity about why those choices are the best possible ones
 ✧ And only then Criteria for how to achieve these results

Of course, the Strategic Alignment Process™ recognizes that you must start with Vision and Mission in order to get to high quality Goals and Strategies. Any other approach will produce a very weak basis for your decision-making.

Inevitably, this is why cracks quickly appear in the results of many traditional strategic planning processes. Look at your last few sessions and see if you have had to work to keep the agreements in place after the meeting. That is your first indication that your process and results are going to be inadequate to achieve the level of real progress, high quality decision-making, and results you would love to have.

THE IMPORTANCE OF QUALITY OF PROCESS

Do you see why a process that distills your team's best thinking in an efficient, effective, and energizing way really matters? **The process must bring out the best in everyone's thinking, while still elevating the dialogue and decisions to the highest common denominator level of team consensus.** Nothing less than that will provide a foundation for keeping everyone in alignment with the decisions. It takes this kind of highly integrated, principle-based, proven process to provide the level of openness, opportunity, and constructive dialogue to ultimately and cleanly get real consensus. It is critical to have a process where productive dialogue raises the quality of the final decisions. Otherwise, you get resignation and frustration that derails true team engagement, agreement.

Look at your last few strategic planning sessions and see if you really believe people provided their best, most honest, and truly committed agreement. If you cannot say your meeting actually produced that, your process is one of the reasons why the agreements coming out of those meetings turned out to be unsustainable.

Here is how the Strategic Alignment Process™ works to generate the kind of dialogue that leads to real and sustainable agreement:

- ✧ Outcomes are clear, stated up front, and guaranteed
- ✧ There is no uncertainty about what everyone is coming together for– and how what they will be doing will influence any decisions
- ✧ The process itself provides a continuously engaging experience that reinforces positive and uplifting from the beginning to the end
- ✧ The participants begin experiencing positive involvement and engagement right from the start.

With the clarity of outcome and quality of process demonstrated throughout the session, people not only relax into what seems like an amazingly natural and engaging flow, **they actually enjoy the experience.** How many of your past meetings do you think your people actually enjoyed, much less got this level of productivity and results?

NEXT STEPS AFTER THE MEETING

The next stage starts immediately after the end of the Strategic Alignment Process™ session. It is essential to put these decisions into action. Building on the quality of momentum that comes out of the Strategic Alignment Process™ requires consistently implementing a few key requirements.

Most fundamentally, the dynamic engagement with the essential building blocks of decision-making need to be tested, maintained, and improved whenever necessary. There is a massive difference between having your Vision, Mission, and Goals on the walls of your offices versus in people's , head, and This is the difference between just handing out a business card at a networking event and having your people be the biggest advocates, promoters, and walking advertisements for your organization.

By embodying the Vision, Mission, and Values, focusing on the Goals, and working to implement the Strategies, your people great decision makers themselves. They can easily test every decision against the most important **what** and **why**, making it simple to choose the appropriate **how** to achieve their Goals.

Leaders are often amazed that the congruence of the Strategic Alignment Process™ gives their people a superior level of engagement, commitment, responsibility, and resourcefulness. Aren't these among the most valuable and desired results a leader wants from the team and the organization?

Maximum success comes from keeping the key elements of the process front and center until they are so inculcated in your people that they are fully alive and present. This takes consistent practice, reminders, and evaluation of how they are doing in making progress.

The best way to ingrain these decision-making criteria is to repeat them until everyone has them embedded in their minds, and they become the basis of all decision-making. Consider opening every meeting with 30 to 40 seconds dedicated to inspiring everyone by reading– with passion – the Vision, Mission, and Values. You follow that up by reviewing the top 3 Goals and then discussing these questions with your team. Whether you run a small operational group, a division, or the whole organization, you start your key team meetings by asking:

- ✧ "Are our Goals still relevant and meaningful measurements of accomplishment of our Vision and Mission?"
  - ○ If the answer is yes, move on to the Strategy questions...
  - ○ If the answer is no, ask, "What improvements are necessary to bring these into alignment?"
- ✧ "How are we doing at making progress towards accomplishing these Goals"
  - ○ If the responses are positive and the benchmarks of progress are being met, move onto the rest of the meeting
  - ○ If the response is negative and the benchmarks of progress are being missed, a discussion about what is needed to fix the situation and improve the outcomes is in order

This kind of reminder, reinforcement, and repetition requires only 1 to 5 minutes at the front end of a meeting. However, it is the fastest, best, and most efficient way of embedding these decision-making foundations across your organization. The power of doing this with your people and teams pays off short- and long-term by:

- ✧ Creating consistent, strong, broad-based focus on what really matters
- ✧ Keeping alive the dynamic engagement with these important points worthy of consistent attention
- ✧ Empowering your people with a clear and present understanding about why these priority objectives matter.

Having these valuable points of reference, your people are in the best possible position for taking ownership of and responsibility for making results happen. Again, what most leaders dream about seeing in their organization is accessible, doable, and profound in its impact.

CHAPTER 14

BUILDING YOUR COMPELLING FUTURE

"Focus on the critical few, not the insignificant many."
Anonymous

Imagine that you have experienced the success of a Strategic Alignment Process™ session with your leadership team. A month reminding everyone about what to focus on, and why it matters, has generated agreement, alignment, and action congruent with your Vision, Mission, Values, and Goals. Now you want to embed this dynamism for the long term, and utilize inertia when it is on your side, building on your momentum.

Here are some key lessons to maintain that momentum through best practices that will allow you to reap the full rewards of the Strategic Alignment Process™:

⬥ Keeping momentum going for the long-term requires consistency of practice

⬥ Maintaining consistency of practice requires persistence in setting expectations

⬥ Building intensity of practices is a powerful driver of impact and effectiveness

⬥ Spreading enthusiasm and engagement throughout your organization is better than having it always from the top

In practical terms what all of these best practices add up to is to see your people taking ownership of the lessons and messages of the Strategic Alignment Process. You want to make sure the understanding and implementation permeates every level of the organization. Kindling the passion for reinforcement of the Vision, Mission, Values, and Goals breeds continuity and sustainability. The stronger the broad-based engagement, the more powerfully these foundations of decision-making will drive your organization.

Here are specific suggestions for implementing all of these aspects of the Strategic Alignment Process™:

1. For the 90 days after your Strategic Alignment Process™ session, insist that every meeting start with a reading of the Vision, Mission, Values, and Goals, as noted above

2. If your organization is large, consider having each division or major group build their own Strategic Alignment Process™ outcomes – the division's Vision, Mission, Values, and Goals that align with and support the overall organizational decision-making

3. At least one of your leadership team meetings a month needs to be a strategic review session, which has to include:
    a. Reviewing what is working well in making progress towards the Goals, and confirming that they are still supporting the fulfillment of the Vision and Mission
    b. Reviewing what the biggest challenges or obstacles to achieving the Goals, and fulfilling the Vision and Mission
    c. Deciding what may need to shift, change or be revised to maintain alignment with the Vision, Mission, Values, and Goals; almost all of these changes should be at the level of Strategies and Goals

4. Have a Strategic Alignment Process™ update session at least quarterly. This is the opportunity to make any updates, revisions, or improvements to the overall plan. This can be a larger group than your usual leadership team, which can serve to keep the organization in tune, aligned, and providing insight and input that may be highly useful

a. In a 3-hour meeting, review all of the key elements to ensure that they are still relevant, accurate, and reflect the most current best thinking and knowledge of the group. Improvements are always welcome, and demonstrate engagement with the content

b. An update of accomplishments, learnings, and where improvement has really taken hold is valuable for motivating and inspiring people

c. Additionally, this is one of the many places for re-grounding everyone in the core decision-making principles and discussing how they are playing out with everyone

d. This is the kind of meeting that is useful for considering future scenario planning and determining what might need additional attention, revision, or acceleration

5. Have Town Hall or organization-wide meetings that include a regular review of the Vision, Mission, Values, and Goals, and solicit questions, perspectives, and issues from your employees

a. Allocating a regular portion of your Town Hall meetings to the Strategic Alignment Process™ output keeps it alive, dynamic, and fully in focus with your organization

i. A good place to start your meetings is to devote a few minutes (5 to 10) to reinforce the importance of the Vision, Mission, Values, and Goals

ii. Highlighting successes, including deepening the organization's successful adoption and congruence with the Vision, Mission, Values, and Goals is also highly effective

6. Embedding the Vision, Mission, and Values in the organizational will give you a good pulse on how strongly they are taking hold across your company.

a. Once the Strategic Alignment Process™ has been set into motion, it is valuable to gauge how:

i. Well the decision-making elements are understood

ii. Consistently these decision-making elements are being used as primary criteria for the choices being made across the company

    iii.   rank and file improvements have been suggested

        1.   Being open to improvements and solutions is one of the best ways to encourage deeper thinking and more taking of responsibility across your organization

    iv.   Whether they see their leaders, managers, and others in authority acting congruently with the Vision, Mission, Values, and Goals

When you accept and build on the important principle of being open to anyone offering suggestions for improvement and/or options for solving important issues, suggesting that the Vision, Mission, Values, and Goals are extremely useful starting points has many advantages, including:

- ✧ Keeping the focus on these primary decision-making elements
- ✧ Improving the likelihood that what people suggest will have greater utility and usefulness
- ✧ Maintaining these critical elements as central frameworks to include in all key decisions

The more focused and embedded the Strategic Alignment Process™ decision-making elements are, the clearer, faster, and more effective your and organization's ability to think and decide will be.

    This is truly the most powerful launching point for everything that matters in advancing the success of your organization!

ADDENDUM – WHAT COMES NEXT?

"Let the beauty of what you love be what you do."
Rumi (13th Century Sufi Poet)

Nothing says you have a well-led organization more than having everyone – from senior management to front-line workers – in alignment around the Vision, Mission, Values, and Goals. These are the decision-making criteria for maximizing success, growth, and sustainability.

When these decision-making foundations are internalized and actualized, you will have an organization that uses significantly more of its energy, resources, and people in the best possible ways. That means focusing on accelerating and elevating growth and success.

When big or small changes in Strategy or tactics need to be made, having a solid platform for decision-making makes these adjustments much simpler and faster. It becomes more like trimming of the sails of a racing sailboat than trying to change the direction of an aircraft carrier. Turning an aircraft carrier is what change management often feels like in most organizations. You have a completely different level of flexibility, adaptability, and openness for your people to make necessary adjustments.

Stability of the primary foundations of decision-making is critically important and valuable. Aligning of the Vision, Mission, Values, and Goals makes it so much easier for your people to understand why changes may be needed. It is also so much simpler to get them to accept and even advocate for appropriate adjustments to maintain alignment.

When your people are clear, focused, and invested in fulfilling the Vision, Mission, and Values and achieving the Goals – the quality of engagement and reduction of resistance is profound.

That is not common in many organizations for the very reasons stated in the first page of leadership does not have agreement with a Vision, Mission, and Goals. Without this, you are operating at a fraction of what is possible. Applying the Strategic Alignment Process™ offers you the way to attain an exceptional level of engagement, performance and meaningful results.

I wish you great success in making the most of these simple and powerfully productive principles. You can always reach out with questions about the Strategic Alignment Process™ at Info@OptimizeIntl.com. You are always welcome to contact us for a free conversation to see what it would take to accelerate and elevate the success of your leadership team and organization.

May your Strategic Alignment serve you well in achieving all that you, your teams, and your organization are capable of!

ACKNOWLEDGEMENTS

"Each player must accept the cards life deals him or her;
but once they are in hand, he or she alone must decide
how to play to cards in order to win the game."

Voltaire

I am so grateful for "the cards that life has dealt me," which to me are reflected best in the people who have graced, guided, challenged, supported, and enhanced my own life, and especially my personal and professional growth and development. What follows is but a partial list of those to whom I am indebted. Please know that I honor and have immense gratitude for every one of you who has made an impact on my life and journey.

My mother was a force of nature who managed to make the household and lives of the 5 males she lived with work amazingly well. She was my first leadership mentor.

The masters of their domains who taught me so much about life, learning, and leadership were an invaluable and irreplaceable part of my journey. Dr James Tin Yua So, Fernando Flores, Stuart Heller, and Tony Robbins all taught me so much that significantly deepened my awareness, understanding, and my own insights. The deep spiritual truths and consciousness about what being a full human being is that was learned at the feet of Baba Muktananda and Gurumayi Chidvila-sananda gave me the deepest sense of purpose and possibilities for my life. In addition to these great masters who have transformed their fields and me so profoundly, I am so fortunate to have been mentored and coached by some of the most amazing professionals I have ever known. With great gratitude I salute Ted Edwards Sr., Alan Weiss, Mark LeBlanc, and Janet Brides.

I am where I am because of the clients who have trusted me in supporting their leadership journeys, development, and desire to deliver the most meaningful impact in their lives and for their organizations. They have challenged me to grow, and made a massive impact on my own learning, development, and ability to bring these transformational leadership principles and practices to fruition. There are more clients I owe thanks to than can be named here, but some who must be acknowledged for their lasting impact on my life and professional work include: Tony Candito, Greg Ross, Rich Holbrook, Nancy Stager, Bob Rivers, Julie Chang, Joe Mechlinski, Cynthia Carpenter, Basil Denno, Marcia Mendes d'Abrue, Michael and Elaine Ward, Jim Cowden, Barri Rafferty, and Tracy Nelson. Thank you hardly seems like enough.

My friends have made my life richer and more wonderful than I could have imagined. The great gift of being both dear friends and wonderful professional collaborators has been an extraordinary joy I have shared with Mitchell Stevko, Ted Edwards Jr., Thomas Benton, Meredith Kimbell, Judi Spear, Susan Mayginnes, Neha Sangwan, and Raj Sisodia. To my oldest friends going back decades – Justin Fallon, Ron Bernstein, Jeremy Seligman, and Rich Margil – I am so grateful for all you have meant to me. You have been so important in sharing so many great adventures and joys of living and learning. A very heartfelt thank you.

For all the exceptional people I have been influenced by, my family stands out in my life. My amazing wife Terri has taught me so much with her generosity of spirit, kindness and caring for everyone who crosses her path, and remarkable common sense. Your love and support lifts up my life in so many ways. I appreciate that you maintain your sense of humor even as I challenge boundaries and norms, and repeat favorite jokes. My remarkable children Julie, Jenn, Dave, and

Harry dazzle me. I marvel at the adults they have become and the impact they are having in their work and lives. They inspire me deeply in the way each of them is committed to making the world a much better place. They continue to challenge my thinking and open new considerations about what living a great life can be. They and their amazing partners in life have learned well how to live from a wise and loving place. The joy and bonds we share as a family are beyond wonderful and uplifting.

My three assistants have been instrumental in supporting my ability to do what I love most – while ensuring the office, business, and I keep running smoothly. Thank you Nancy Costa, Jennifer Miceli, and Stephanie Streeter – you know how much I appreciate each one of you.

Finally, thank you dear reader, for engaging in this transformational process of making much better decisions. Let's continue to work together in the service of elevating leaders committed to building better organizations that make a bigger difference in the lives of their people, clients, communities, and the world.

ABOUT THE AUTHOR – STEVE LISHANSKY

Steve Lishansky works with CEOs, CIO's, C-Suite leaders, and their teams as an executive coach and strategic mentor to drive leadership team performance and organizational results. His leaders find they make higher quality decisions faster, align their organizations better, improve their prioritization efficiency, and deliver outstanding results more consistently.

Steve founded and led 2 fast-growing, multi-million-dollar companies prior to founding his leadership and executive coaching company Optimize International in 1992. As an executive coach, professional speaker, strategic decision-making facilitator, and best-selling author, Steve works with talented and successful leaders to better leverage their talents, capabilities, and resources in delivering the greatest impact and results.

He coaches C-Suite and senior leadership teams to work together better, agree on top priorities faster, and more congruently communicate and achieve what really matters. That produces leaders who grow their business faster, develop their people better, and sustainably increase their value to their clients and communities.

His clients have included: Accenture, PricewaterhouseCoopers, Deloitte, The FAA, NASA, Johnson & Johnson, Novartis, Novo Nordisk, The Clinic by Cleveland Clinic, Fidelity, MetLife, State Street, eTrade, Cisco, EMC, Oakley and fast growth entrepreneurial companies. Steve thrives on his family, global travel adventures, meditation, health and fitness, mentoring young people, and making a significant and sustainable difference in the world.

Contact: Info@OptimizeIntl.com
www.OptimizeIntl.com
978-369-4525

www.ingramcontent.com/pod-product-compliance
Lightning Source LLC
Chambersburg PA
CBHW072200270326
41930CB00011B/2497